MW00829846

The Gift of Travel

Travel

Passport to Mindfulness, Gratitude, and Compassion!

Michael Lladó-Dávila

The Gift of Travel: Passport to Mindfulness, Gratitude and Compassion!

Copyright © 2022 by Michael Lladó-Dávila

All rights reserved. No part of this publication may be reproduced, distributed, or transmitted in any form or by any means, including photocopying, recording, or other electronic or mechanical methods, without the prior written permission of the publisher, except in the case of brief quotations embodied in critical reviews and certain other noncommercial uses permitted by copyright law.

Published by Michael Lladó-Dávila

Cover Design and Layout by Timothy Scott

A CIP record for this book is available from the Library of Congress Cataloging-in-Publication Data

ISBN: 978-0-578-38625-6 (Print)
ISBN: 979-8-9859190-0-4 (E-Book)

Website: Llado-Davila.com

Dedication

For my wife, Claudia, and our daughter, Lindsey. You both have taught me so much about the gifts of being present, gratefulness, and compassion. I love you both so very much. May the Harmonious Trio, guided by our eternal God, be forever in your lives!

Contents

Acknowledgments

This undertaking wouldn't have been possible without Divine inspiration and the aggregate wisdom of people believing in what I could accomplish.

Although I didn't thank him at the time, I'm forever grateful to Robert Doyle, my English teacher during my junior and senior years at St. Helena's High School in New York City. Sir, you instilled in me a profound appreciation for art and literature. I'll be eternally grateful!

I'm also thankful to Drs. Aruna Michie, Phillip Althoff, John Keller, and John Selfridge, truly dedicated and outstanding professors at Kansas State University, where I attended graduate school. They showed me how to believe in myself and have faith in what I could achieve. I'll always be indebted to them for nourishing the seeds of critical thinking.

As one of my editors and proofreaders, Nathan Hipps, emphasized that patience and persistence are extremely vital to the writing process. He also introduced me to one of Tallahassee's favorite eating establishments, where we nourished ourselves with discussions of fine writing and excellent cuisine. Consequently, my appetite for tasty food and clear, concise wordsmithing flourished. I thank Nathan for welcoming me to a new adventure.

My deep appreciation also goes to Nicolette Costantino, another of my copy editors and proofreaders. Nicolette personified the true essence of mindfulness, gratefulness, and compassion simply by being herself. Because of her dedication and devotion to these attributes, my commitment to them intensified even more. Her feedback also led to a deeper appreciation of the writing process and energized my commitment to express myself peacefully without fearing what others might say.

Special thanks also go to Timothy Scott of TS Media/Designs who designed this book. The front and back covers are exquisite! His patience with a novice writer greatly eased the process.

A sincere and special thanks to these individuals for planting and watering the seeds of mindfulness, gratitude, and compassion!

Opening Words

The genesis for *The Gift of Travel* originated during an overseas trip I took with my wife and daughter in 2016. Because of this journey, I learned to look at travel and daily living through the lenses of mindfulness, gratefulness, and compassion. These attributes added immense value to our experience.

Throughout our Holiday, I reflected on many art forms and places visited. By mindfully immersing myself in these opportunities, I was deeply thankful for how noted artists, writers, scholars, and others from years past communed with me centuries later. Indeed, their works allowed me to explore many aspects of my life experiences, thereby, enriching my personal and spiritual development.

I also learned that connecting with the past enables us to intensify our appreciation for the present. However, it's imperative not to enslave ourselves to life's adversities; otherwise, we won't flourish as individuals. Counterbalancing our trials and tribulations with special tender, loving moments of our lives is essential. In short, this book is part travel memoir and part autobiography. Perhaps it may be referred to as a *"Travelagraphy."* How's that for combining writing genres!

When writing about my experiences, journaling became a close, dear friend, enabling me to contemplate discoveries about myself, while simultaneously integrating memories of the places we visited, people we met, and the love and laughter I shared with my wife and daughter. These memories continue to nourish our growth as a family and remind me that we're all members of one family. For this, I'm eternally grateful!

Introduction

The powdery, flowing snow-covered landscapes of France, Germany, Austria, and Italy and the vibrant history of each country were magical and transformational. My 2016 Christmas holiday with the two loves of my life exceeded expectations for appreciating and immersing myself in such a glorious season. With each passing day of our journey, I realized my perspective on traveling and meeting different people was metamorphosing into a "harmonious trio" of heightened mindfulness, gratitude, and compassion. This renewed mindset continues to enrich my mental, emotional, physical, and spiritual well-being. Who knew traveling overseas would foster such meaningful change at the age of sixty-three?

Before the trip, my wife, Claudia, our daughter, Lindsey, and I had traveled throughout the United States and other countries. However, self-imposed obstacles detracted from fully appreciating the places we visited and the people we met. Preoccupation with others' behaviors, long waiting lines, workplace assignments, sticking to our itinerary, and other self-imposed obstacles limited my ability to delight in the here-and-now. Upon returning home to Tallahassee, Florida, I acted like a caged hamster going round and round on my spinning wheel. Like a robot, I indulged in mindlessly unpacking, doing house chores, washing clothes, going shopping, and other activities. Sadly, I was not as mindful and thankful as I should have been for having the opportunity to travel with Claudia and Lindsey and develop a greater consciousness of myself and the world around me.

Travel resources emphasize sightseeing, physical activities like skiing and hiking, and relaxation. In addition, they offer essential information on when to visit certain countries, passport and visa requirements, where to eat and stay, exchange rates, car rentals, discounts, and other topics. Resources on eco-tours and education tours show how they open doors to new opportunities. For example, eco-tours allow travelers to visit pristine natural environments worldwide, while education tours enable participants to learn about diverse cultures and languages. Although planning to enjoy cultural, historical, and scenic highlights is vital, there seems to be a crucial missing link in travel resources. They don't explain how our immersion in unfamiliar cultures and lifestyles can lead to a deeper understanding and appreciation of self and others.

Instead, we often constrain ourselves when traveling and insist on staying within our comfort zone. Consequently, we do not overcome negative prejudices and biases resulting from cultural, religious, and other differences. Traveling may even worsen these negativities if we experience them outside our social and cultural norms. Moreover, personality traits may inhibit being open to others and learning from them. The harmonious trio increased my understanding of how we're interconnected physically, emotionally, and spiritually.

If we appreciate and value this linkage, we can expand our level of consciousness and nurture our ability to engage others peaceably despite any differences.

Before continuing further, I'll show how the daily practice of mindfulness, gratitude, and compassion leads to a lifestyle devoid of mentally, emotionally, and physically abusing ourselves and others. A mindset emphasizing the harmonious trio leads to inner and outer peace, thus resulting in greater awareness and appreciation of ourselves, others, and our surroundings.

Mindfulness

Mindfulness centers on the here and now without judging it as good or bad. It requires being keenly aware of what we're experiencing and grounding ourselves in the present. As I'm writing, I'm focused on my thoughts and in tune with expressing myself as clearly and concisely as possible. I'm not allowing competing ideas to dominate my mind, such as work commitments, errands, doctors' appointments, laundry, washing my car, working out, wondering what to eat, what to wear, etc. I'm not regretting I should have pursued writing and other areas of interest earlier in my life. The chirping birds outside my office window offer a soothing, melodic background complimenting my efforts without distractions. However, the present, or the here and now, often includes appreciating and respecting past events, which I'll describe in later sections.

During childhood, I didn't understand the importance of living in the present. Thoughts unrelated to the subject or activity at hand throughout my education often sidetracked me. Usually, my mind focused on playing baseball and running track, two of my favorite sports. I also could have paid closer attention to work projects and my interaction with co-workers during my professional career. At times, while talking to a colleague about a critical assignment, I thought about the Mets' baseball score the night before and whether they'd win the pennant (they usually don't!). On other occasions, while spending time with loved ones, I thought about an upcoming business trip rather than giving them one hundred percent of my attention. My failure to concentrate on the present undermined thoroughly appreciating and respecting special moments. Being mindful requires long-term commitment and dedication to its practice; it's not an overnight process. In my case, I gently remind myself to practice being in the present daily.

Specific experiences in the mid-1990s planted the seeds for mindful living. While visiting a local public library, I inadvertently found books on mindfulness, which piqued my interest. I soon discovered the practice is rooted in centuries-old Eastern traditions where meditation plays a vital role. In the U.S., studies of effective mindfulness techniques encompass scientific, empirical, and spiritual approaches, in addition to yoga, meditation, and breathing exercises. Since the 1970s, mindfulness programs addressing depression, stress, drug addiction, anxiety, aging, body weight, and other areas have gained momentum in prisons, schools, businesses, and medical centers.

Before the trip, I reread Henry David Thoreau's *Walden*, published in 1852. Although it has been my favorite book since college, rereading it enriched my appreciation of living in the present. In writing about his experience at Walden Pond, Thoreau meticulously described the picturesque surroundings, including the sounds of nature and wildlife. As his words created vivid images in my mind, I remembered the books I'd read on mindfulness years before.

Walden influenced my decision to practice being present while traveling. I sincerely felt experiencing the now would heighten my experience and magnify spending quality time with Claudia and Lindsey. I'm still unsure why I chose to emulate Thoreau and his commitment to contemplate the present, or the now, for this trip and not earlier ones. Perhaps, subconsciously, I thought of how he touched the lives of millions of people, including Mahatma Gandhi, Martin Luther King, and the Dalai Lama. Maybe, I also wanted to experience the now and see what I could learn from it.

Beginning with our first day in Paris, I made a conscious effort to concentrate on whatever I experienced at any moment, such as studying paintings, sculptures, buildings, and monuments. Being present and alert also deepened my eagerness to communicate with individuals, including discussing an artwork, piece of music, or place visited. These interactions enabled me to connect with others, regardless of cultural and other differences, leading to a more in-depth, happier travel experience.

Since our return, I've used the practice of being mindful when interacting with others, even when we have differing opinions. Little or no knowledge of what a friend, acquaintance, or business associate has experienced often results in misunderstandings and conflict. Possibly they've been verbally, emotionally, or physically abused by a loved one, thus influencing a particular behavior or belief. Perhaps the individual was unjustly fired from a job, resulting in a negative view of authority figures. Because of these unknowns, I shouldn't prejudge others. Otherwise, I may fail to understand and appreciate their rationale for personal beliefs and behaviors. Indeed, it is vital to focus on the present without judging it as good or bad.

In some instances, the present moment may involve unfortunate events, such as the passing of a loved one or a severe accident involving a family member. Rather than running from these realities or hiding our emotions, we need to face and learn from them. If we allow sorrowful moments to be transformative, addressing future challenges may be less stressful.

Mindfulness and Meditation

Daily meditation has increased my awareness of feelings, thoughts, actions, and surroundings. Also, it positively affects how I communicate with others since my ability to remain attentive has improved dramatically. Interestingly, researchers have found that mindfulness training and meditation positively influence those parts of the brain involving attention, emotion, and self-awareness. Therefore, both practices can significantly improve our well-being and quality of life.

Various resources teach how to practice different meditation strategies. I favored focused meditation throughout the trip and continue to employ it daily. Through it, I concentrate on breathing, a specific object, activity, or thought. Frequently, I might listen to a classical piece of music, smell the scent of a burning candle, or look at pictures taken during a family trip. If my mind wanders while meditating, I redirect it back to my focus. One of my favorite meditation strategies centers on breathing. I breathe in and out through my nose and abandon whatever thoughts come to mind. Meditating first thing in the morning in a comfortable, upright pose and quiet atmosphere stimulates clarity of mind and emotional serenity. It helps pave the way to appreciating and performing daily tasks, however strenuous or challenging. Usually, I meditate for twenty to thirty minutes. If I get stressed or anxious during the day, I do a brief breathing exercise, thereby stimulating mental and emotional tranquility.

Gratitude

Mindfulness creates space for valuing and appreciating myself, others, and the world around me. There are many ways to express thankfulness and nurture greater happiness and better health. For instance, studies show that being grateful helps control blood pressure without medication; also, it promotes restful sleep. Unfortunately, I've often taken ways of expressing thankfulness for granted. Beginning with our stay in Paris, I appreciated how the paintings and sculptures in museums added depth to my enjoyment. I also made a concerted effort to thank the staff at hotels, restaurants, museums, tours, trains, and other areas for their help and smiles. These simple acts increased gladness and well-being as others reciprocated with grins and kindness. A simple smile transcended cultural and language barriers; indeed, we all smile in the same language!

These humble gestures reminded me of a mission trip I took to Cuenca, Ecuador, in 1995. While there, I watched gratitude in action. My group's primary goal was to pour a concrete foundation for a new house of worship in an impoverished neighborhood. Sadly, some local church members wore tattered clothing, shoes, and sandals. In addition to having limited access to nutritional food and health care, several homes had no heat or air conditioning. Yet, I've never seen the degree of joy and happiness these folks exuded despite their situation.

When mingling with them, I realized they were grateful for what they had and didn't complain about what they didn't have. As my mission group helped pour a concrete foundation, they helped me build the groundwork for expressing thankfulness for the blessings in my life, big and small. They also revealed how mindfulness and gratitude work in harmony with compassion. While helping lay the church's foundation, they labored to the best of their ability and were grateful for the mission group's help. Church members also cared for the impoverished elderly of their community at nighttime.

Compassion

Throughout our travel, I often sat in the hotel lobby. I liked watching others as they checked in or out of the hotel, waited for family and friends, or pursued other activities. In many instances, parents hugged and played with their children reminding me of similar experiences with Lindsey. Fondly remembering these loving moments, I exchanged smiles and laughter with families, reminding me of our shared humanity regardless of our differences. Small moments like these can also lead to helping others in times of need because we're elevating our ability to exude kindness, compassion's worthy companion.

Actively and mindfully listening to others during the trip also rekindled my passion for resolving interpersonal conflict. Since the trip, I've resumed helping others with my conflict resolution and anger management skills. As a result, I've developed greater sensitivity toward others while helping to resolve some of their issues. After all, the challenges I've faced reflect those of most individuals, including having enough money for food, shelter, transportation, health care, and other necessities. In addition, emotional and mental issues emanating from our childhood may affect how we treat ourselves and others. This reality significantly amplifies my willingness and commitment to being sensitive and responsive to others' needs, including feeling empathy for another's misfortune, such as losing a job or a loved one.

Recently, I comforted an elderly couple from Tallahassee whose son had recently died. By expressing deep sympathy and helping them in whatever way I could, I felt an emotional and spiritual uplift by serving them and not expecting, or wanting, anything in return. Despite our political differences, I also asked myself how I would feel under similar circumstances. Soon, I felt a sense of freedom because I've often judged individuals whose beliefs and opinions differ from mine. My willingness to help the couple cope with their travesty and involve myself in their suffering increased immeasurably. This renewed mindset continues to reach out to others. It's been so fruitful stepping out of my old comfort zone and freeing myself from negative biases and prejudices.

Trying to ease others' suffering has intensified my willingness to show compassion toward them. Self-compassion also plays a crucial role in how we treat ourselves. Since the trip, I've been practicing being kind to myself and mindful that, at times, I do not meet my needs and the needs of others. During my career, I traveled much because of work requirements when Lindsey was young. As a result, spending quality time with her was significantly reduced. Also, I often worked late at night when I could have been at home with my family. As Lindsey grew older, I became angry, thinking I'd neglected her. However, that had never been my intention. Fortunately, I've learned to forgive and be kind to myself, promoting a healthier mindset.

Undeniably, compassion positively affects our well-being and quality of life because it enables us to empathize with others and see life through their eyes and not ours. However, caring for others can result in emotional, physical, and spiritual stress and exhaustion. Doctors, nurses, and others in the caring professions may suffer because of experiencing death or serious illnesses regularly. These adversities can affect their work performance, how they relate to others, and a host of other negative behaviors. Fortunately, there're resources to help individuals experiencing compassion fatigue.

Leading researchers employing secular approaches to studying mindfulness, gratitude, and compassion include John Kabat-Zinn, Ellen J. Langer, John Kralik, Kristi Nelson, Kristin Neff, and Christopher Germer. In addition, prominent individuals who embrace and convey the spiritual nature of these three attributes are the 14th Dalai Lama, Thich Nhat Hanh, Thomas Keating, Eckhart Tolle, Cynthia Bourgeault, and Richard Rohr.

Why Journaling is a Good Friend

Before our 2016 trip, vacations and other excursions helped create fond memories, even if I didn't actively indulge in practicing mindfulness, gratitude, and compassion. I recently flipped through an album having pictures of vacations I took with my parents as a child. Still, I faintly remember why we took those trips. However, if I'd kept a journal, I would better recollect where we visited and what I learned.

Before leaving the U.S., I decided to journal and document our overseas flights, the places we visited, what we ate, and what I felt and learned on any given day. Thoreau's *Walden* influenced my decision because he journaled about his Walden Pond experience. Journaling soon became a good friend who inspired me to develop my concept of the harmonious trio.

During our first full day in Paris, I wrote about the previous day's activities. Then, as I waited for my two sleepy heads to join me for breakfast, I contemplated what I had written, deepening my commitment to the here and now. Joyfully, I felt a sense of renewal!

Simultaneously, I was incredibly grateful to travel overseas with my wife and daughter and exercise mindfulness. Soon thereafter, I experienced an aha moment! I could express how showing gratitude whenever possible increases the happiness resulting from travel and other areas of our lives.

Thankfully, I also thought of Notre Dame Cathedral's nativities, wreaths, and other decorations exuding love, kindness, and forgiveness. In addition, miniature villages depicted people communing with one another in a spirit of Christmas joy and kind-heartedness. Soon, I smiled, recognizing I had the beginnings of a book's thesis! I could look at our journey through heightened mindfulness, gratitude, and compassion and how they stimulate personal renewal and transformation. The harmonious trio's birth was an early Christmas blessing and impetus for writing a travel memoir!

Throughout our journey, journaling, and the thoughts it engendered, added vigor to my overseas experience. It expanded my ability and commitment to writing about our sightseeing, meeting people, and what I learned about myself and others. A lifelong transformation was taking place!

Because of Europe's rich history, I also wrote about how past events impact today. If it hadn't been for the heroic deeds of soldiers, pilots, nurses, and other individuals during World Wars, we wouldn't have the freedom to visit these places today. Because of the bombing raids, which destroyed significant parts of European cities in World War II, the decision to reconstruct them after the war intensified my eagerness to value and learn about their history. Journaling also enabled me to reflect on our ability to overcome life's tragedies. Indeed, I gained a deeper appreciation of people's dedication and commitment to keeping history alive.

Since returning from our trip, I've continued to journal daily. I reflect on whatever I may have experienced the day before, or whatever comes to mind, as clearly as possible. Hence, I can track my physical, emotional, and spiritual well-being and assess if I'm happy with my progress or lack thereof. Entries also address the unfolding events on national and international scales and the need for the harmonious trio to address serious issues. Finally, journaling also empowers me to show my appreciation and compassion for others and influence the world, even if on a small scale.

Journaling also requires being present because I concentrate on portraying my experience accurately. For example, if I'm writing about cleaning dishes, I focus on how the warm water feels as it touches my hands and how the suds glide off each plate, pan, or utensil. Sometimes, any negativity I experienced during the day also washes away. This simple act, which I learned from the writings of Thich Nhat Hanh, instills calmness, peace of mind, and appreciation for experiencing the present.

I've also begun a gratitude journal because it's a constant reminder to be thankful for everyday life. In it, I write three to five things I'm grateful for, two to three times weekly; others make daily entries. My entries are as specific as possible. I write about being thankful for my home, meeting people, clear night skies, healthy food to eat, and the special bond Claudia and I have with Lindsey. Because of these gifts, I'll always welcome them. I especially enjoy looking at night stars and cannot fathom ever taking them for granted. As a child, I remember appreciating these treasured gems amid the impoverished neighborhood where I lived. Undoubtedly, they were a welcome reprieve from neighborhood blight.

Before our overseas trip, family getaways enabled me to enjoy people, gorgeous scenery, stunning architecture, food, and other whatnots. Although this led to exciting and fantastic experiences with Claudia and Lindsey, the harmonious trio enriched our 2016 Christmas voyage and furthered self-discovery and personal renewal!

Chapter 1

A Yearn to Travel: It's a Family Thing!

Acknowledging the past affects the present and the present influences the future furthers a better understanding of ourselves and others. Hence, an excellent place to begin writing about our overseas trip is with earlier travel experiences and how they inspired going overseas.

My love for traveling began at an early age. While living in my birthplace of Puerto Rico, my family and I enjoyed many Sunday car rides enabling us to enjoy the island's rolling green hills and majestic, lush mountains touching the sky. When I was six years old, we moved to the Bronx, a borough of New York City. We resumed our Sunday excursions when I was ten years old by driving to Danbury, Connecticut. During the ride, I remembered fond memories of our Sunday travels in Puerto Rico.

What made the outing even happier was my mother's sister, Asyria, and brother, Ruben, accompanying us. Their presence resulted in a memorable family get-together, highlighted by laughter and memories of their childhood. Because their father died when they were young, they affectionately recalled the challenges of being raised by a single parent.

Although Sunday travel bestowed fond memories, I was often pre-occupied with homework assignments, class projects, track meets, baseball games, and other activities consuming the upcoming week. As a result, I often overlooked the beautiful countryside outside our car windows. Because of an abundant love for clouds, I could have nourished a greater appreciation of them. In addition, spending quality time talking with my father, Miguel, and mother, Myrna, would have deepened a greater appreciation of their life experiences.

Since Claudia and I met in high school in 1970, we've enjoyed and craved traveling. After marrying in 1972, at an early age (Claudia was eighteen and I was nineteen), we traveled in our 1972 Volkswagen Super Beetle throughout New York, Canada, New England, and several southern states. We liked camping in a small green pup tent wherever we went. However, when it rained, we became one with the universe outside. Tiny raindrops dripping from the tent's seams refreshed our spirits while smiling at each other.

One of our favorite weekend escapes was Walden Pond in Massachusetts, about a three-hour drive from NYC. I remember reading Henry David Thoreau's *Walden* and how it created vibrant images, thus embellishing our visits to the pond. His book came alive as Claudia, and I floated in our inflatable rubber raft while communing with the water's tranquility. Admiring the moon, stars, and sunrise enriched our experience immensely. Little did I know fond memories of our immersion in Walden's beauty and serenity would resurface as I began journeying through the practice of mindfulness. However, as I recollect these trips, I'm reminded they often competed with self-imposed distractions, such as thinking about work and school projects, doing laundry, grocery shopping, exercising, and other activities. Sadly, these hindrances continued throughout a good part of adulthood.

Although Claudia and I enjoyed traveling, we usually had time constraints and didn't engage ourselves fully in the places we visited. I remember a weekend excursion we took to the Canadian side of Niagara Falls. I picked Claudia up on a Friday afternoon at her workplace in downtown NYC and drove eight hours to Niagara Falls. Because our visit encompassed mindlessly rushing from one attraction to another, we didn't fully appreciate the Falls' beauty and magnificence. On Sunday, we returned home to the Bronx, and upon entering our apartment, we promptly succumbed to the seduction of sleep. We woke up at six o'clock the following day to the sound of an overzealous alarm clock and took the subway train to work. Once downtown on Fifth Avenue, a small grocery store in Rockefeller Center welcomed us with tasty cinnamon buns.

After enlisting in the U.S. Army in 1975, Claudia and I traveled to our assignment in Germany. We enjoyed its culture, people, food, and splendor during a two-year tour while also traveling to France, Switzerland, Italy, and Austria. However, tight time schedules, once again, undermined our experience. In addition, I often thought about tasks awaiting me back on post. As in earlier travels, we wanted to see as much as possible and impress ourselves and others with the places we visited. However, just sitting and admiring a sunset or sunrise in Garmisch-Partenkirchen in southern Bavaria, one of our favorite places, would have increased our appreciation and enjoyment of Germany.

While stationed in the U.S., and after being discharged from the military, we traveled throughout the Midwest, Southwest, and West coast. Once again, we wanted to conquer what the world offered as quickly as possible. Thinking back, our insistence on keeping a tight schedule may have been because of NYC's fast pace. In addition, task-oriented teachers surrounded me as a youth. Immediately after doing Task A, we moved on to Task B, and so on. For example, we finished math class in grade school and immediately attended another course. Unfortunately, I often thought about the earlier class because I didn't understand the math teacher's lesson; this worsened matters. After-school tutoring programs would have been helpful.

Claudia, Lindsey, and I fondly remember our trips throughout Florida, Canada, Mexico, New England, Puerto Rico, the Bahamas, and New York. In 2001, we traveled to Canada and visited the enchanted land of Anne of Green Gables in Cavendish, Prince Edward Island. I remember walking from our bungalow to the Gulf of St. Lawrence and relishing how the red sand glistened and blended beautifully into the water. Our nightly ice cream, and a cool summer breeze blowing ever gently on the Gulf of St. Lawrence, will always remain a cherished memory. In retrospect, these experiences may have manifested what I read about mindfulness in the 1990s; however, I didn't realize it at the time.

Lindsey experienced her first overseas travel when Ms. Crow, her kindergarten teacher, took her class on an imaginary trip to Italy. Lindsey was an excited passenger on this incredible adventure! I remember the passport she designed and used when boarding the make-believe plane. I also recall when Claudia and I fed Lindsey's class with food native to Italy. I'll forever be grateful to Ms. Crow for nourishing Lindsey's love of learning and planting seeds for future warm memories of travel.

In 2015, Lindsey explored parts of England on a trip entitled "Jane Austen: Town and Country England Tour." She deepened her knowledge and appreciation of her favorite author throughout the journey while developing a fondness for tea, fish and chips, and other English cuisine. On a side note, enabling Lindsey's love for reading is one of the most profound gifts Claudia and I have given her. Through reading, Lindsey, Claudia, and I have traveled to distant lands, deepening our appreciation and respect for diverse cultures without leaving home.

Now that I'm older and wiser, the harmonious trio of increased mindfulness, gratitude, and compassion magnifies reasons for traveling. In addition to spending time with family and visiting exciting places, I now make a concerted effort to communicate with and learn about others' backgrounds and interests. An expanded mindset deepens an understanding of how we're universally connected despite cultural, racial, and other differences.

There will always be a season to appreciate the interconnectedness we share and how different generations intertwine. For those old enough to remember, the Byrds, a popular band in the 1960s, used Ecclesiastes 3:1-10 when writing lyrics to "Turn! Turn! Turn!" As I recall, it was an exceedingly popular tune touching millions of young people, myself included. The song accentuates the various seasons of our lives, including letting go of hatred and tearing down barriers between people. It also expresses it's never too late to respect and empathize with others and co-exist peacefully. This belief reinforces a personal commitment to practicing mindfulness, gratitude, and compassion daily. Interestingly, when Lindsey was born, "Turn! Turn! Turn!" played on a radio station in Tallahassee. A delightful song connected the beautiful, wondrous experience of Lindsey's birth to my youth and the 1960s generation!

Chapter 2

Planning and Bon Voyage!

While munching on a cheesy, saucy, mouth-watering pizza at a local restaurant, I asked Lindsey how she enjoyed working at a statewide Public Television network. She's been employed there since graduating with a Master's in Communication from Florida State University in 2011. Following her update, she casually suggested we take a European Christmas vacation. She thought we could fly to Paris and then travel to Munich, Venice, and Florence. Of course, this came as no surprise since we often discussed visiting these places.

So, upon hearing her proposal on a hot June summer day, I realized she had invested considerable time thinking about traveling overseas. Later that day, I approached Claudia, and agreeing it was a promising idea, the three of us spent the next few months making travel plans. We perused different resources during summer and fall, including books, guides, maps, and websites. Lindsey prepared a travel itinerary as we identified places to visit and the time to spend in each (if this had been left to me, I'd still be planning it!).

We contacted the American Automobile Association (AAA) Travel Club in Tallahassee to help with travel arrangements. Our representative, Ellen, did a marvelous job scheduling our flight from Orlando International Airport to Paris on December 17 and returning from Florence to Orlando with stopovers in Paris and Atlanta on December 31. She also reserved excellent hotel accommodations for us. Claudia and I booked our flight from Paris to Munich; we also planned our train travel from Munich to Venice and from Venice to Florence.

Before our departure, Claudia, Lindsey, and I brushed up on conversational French, German, and Italian. I must admit the French language, and I don't get along very well; I can't master pronouncing many words. However, I easily refamiliarized myself with German since Claudia and I had lived in Germany for two years. While there, we enriched our ability to speak practical German by visiting gasthauses, which are like inns, taverns, or restaurants. These oases of the local culture are usually family-owned; some even have hotel rooms to rent. Practicing Italian was straightforward because there're similarities between it and Spanish, my native language.

On the day before our morning flight, we drove from Tallahassee to Orlando, registered at our hotel on International Drive, and ate dinner at one of our favorite restaurants within walking distance. While dining, we discussed the itinerary for our first day in the City of Lights, including visiting the Musée d'Orsay, Notre Dame Cathedral, and Shakespeare and Company Bookstore.

Day 1 (Saturday): Overseas Flight

After sleeping a few hours, we awakened at 3:30 am and drove to our morning flight. Once inside the plane, flight attendants energetically delivered snacks, food, and hot towelettes. By the way, this isn't a paid endorsement.

Upon taking off from American soil, our pilot remarked, "Relax and enjoy the flight," to which I thought, "Really? Well, I'll try my best, even though I feel like an oversized sardine in a small 12-ounce can." How sardines enjoy this afterlife so we can eat them is beyond me. Had we been three feet shorter or had retractable legs, we would have had ample legroom and space between seats. Thoreau wrote, "The mass of men lead lives of quiet desperation." Although the context of his writing was different than an overseas flight in quarters meant for sardines, I couldn't help but remember his quote. Because of the tight seating arrangements, I unequivocally experienced "quiet desperation." Thoreau also wrote, "I would rather sit on a pumpkin and have it all to myself than be crowded on a velvet cushion." Boy, do I wish I had sat on a pumpkin with ample leg space between other pumpkins during the flight!

Claudia, Lindsey, and I entertained ourselves by playing video games on tiny screens in front of us, watching sitcoms, tracking our flight, and reading. Of course, we spoke about the thrill of flying overseas and enjoying the places we would soon visit. A baby in front of us crying throughout much of the flight added to our overseas adventure. This ensured that Claudia and I wouldn't nod off for too long. Luckily for Lindsey, she slept for several hours. Later in the day, I remembered when Lindsey, at three months old, cried incessantly on a flight from Jacksonville, Florida, to New York City. I would've been more sensitive to the crying baby and his parents had I remembered this. When the man sitting in front of Claudia reclined his seat, his head almost touched her lap. It seemed as if he wanted to brighten her flight with his bald, highly shined head. Also, because I forgot to chew gum as we took off, it took a while for my ears to pop. The baby's crying may have played a key role in helping them to pop finally. I should have thanked him!

During the flight, I often walked up and down the narrow aisles. While doing so, I noticed people sleeping and snoring with their mouths wide open. Boy, was I jealous! Why couldn't I look as ridiculous as they did? At least I'd be sleeping. Since this wasn't the case, I could have developed a new paradigm for world peace while walking the aisles. Upon returning to my seat, I tried to get as cozy and relaxed as possible, but the confinement of seating arrangements nixed this idea. It seems there should be a law forbidding this cruel and unusual punishment!

As mentioned earlier, flight attendants kept us fed and did their best to address the flight's tediousness. One attendant brought me a drink every 30 minutes throughout a good part of the flight. I started my countdown for the next round of liquid ambrosia after about 20 minutes. As with delivery packages, I considered tracking its travel until it reached my seat, its undisputed destination. It was fun connecting with my new best friend and most fabulous bartender ever! Perhaps he saw my quiet desperation and empathized with me.

Toward the end of the flight, I discovered a channel with peaceful sounds of rain and other watery delights. However, one problem arose. As soon as I got sleepy-eyed, I had to get up for restroom breaks. It's true! The sound of water often makes people "go" more often. My college statistics teacher would have been proud of me. After all, I found a correlation between the sound of water and having to "go." However, I was still unable to calculate the standard deviation and other statistical measures, so it's no wonder I only got a "C" in the class.

Nearing Paris, the baby finally stopped crying. As his mother held him against her chest, he looked right at me. He had an adoring big smile, round face, blond hair, and beautiful blue eyes. While speaking with his father, I learned he was originally from France and lived in the U.S. with his French wife. He worked in information technology, and his spouse was a language teacher at a community college. Both husband and wife listened attentively and smiled as I shared our itinerary in Paris. Then, as his wife held her now quiet pride and joy, the husband recommended times to visit the Eiffel Tower and other iconic places.

During our conversation, I realized I could have created a better atmosphere for learning about others. Instead, I quietly complained to myself and indulged in a pity party because of my perceived discomfort. Also, I was experiencing overseas travel with the two loves of my life. Unfortunately, I wasn't fully mindful of this and other positive experiences I encountered during the flight, resulting in lost opportunities. It was a blessing to watch my wife and daughter in their peaceful short-lived sleep as the baby's cries traveled the universe. God has blessed me with two beautiful gifts: a loving, caring wife puts up with my imperfections, and our daughter exudes her mom's kindness and compassion. Unlike me, Lindsey also sleeps through the furor of loud noises and crying babies!

A brief conversation with my new French acquaintances reminded me that what may seem like inconsequential experiences often create lasting, joyful memories. In addition, I was thankful for bonding with my family during the flight. This connection highlighted simplicity at its finest: we talked about our travel itinerary, played video games, read, poked fun at our tight quarters, and saw Claudia deal with an unwelcome shiny, bald head she hadn't ordered. The three of us still laugh at this memory.

The crying baby also reminded me of Lindsey's younger years and the happiness and joy she brought to me. Claudia's attempt to snag invisible flies as she periodically dozed off evoked fond memories of our marriage and the countless times, I've watched her sleep. I also remembered our first trip to Paris. Because of limited finances, we bought a loaf of bread for breakfast while later experiencing fine French cuisine consisting of hamburgers and fries at a fast-food restaurant close to the Arch of Triumph. I recall laughing and pretending we were part of the bourgeoise as we dined in the City of Lights. After all, two kids from the Bronx were dining in downtown Paris! Our intense feelings, deep affection, and commitment to each other superseded the cost of any fine French wine, even a bottle of Chateau LaFite Rothschild!

Remembrances of small moments form mountains of cherished memories. Their accumulation, especially those of gut-wrenching laughter among the three of us, helped make our 2016 adventure genuinely memorable.

Chapter 3

City of Lights

Day 2 (Sunday)

We were among the last to disembark at Charles de Gaulle International Airport. As we deboarded, I thanked the most generous bartender of all time and the other attendants for a job well done and bid farewell to the *now* sleepy baby and his parents. Then, I looked at the instrument panels and controls in the cockpit. I've always been mesmerized by the hundreds of bright-colored buttons, switches, electronic maps, and other gadgets.

> *After Heathrow in London, Charles de Gaulle International Airport, or Aéroport Paris-Charles-de-Gaulle, is the largest international airport in France and Europe's 2nd busiest. Opened in March 1974, it's named after the former French president, who served from 1959 to 1969.*

The passenger boarding bridge provided an imaginary red-carpet welcome to Paris's magnificence. Soon, we would engage its people, history, and cultural amenities. Upon entering the terminal and its long corridors, I chose not to mindlessly walk from Point A to Point

B, as I did on other occasions when visiting cities for the first time. I didn't want to undermine the newness of my experience. Even though it was early, hundreds of travelers hurried from place to place as airport personnel gave directions to destinations. Individuals with headphones and Bluetooths growing out of their ears must have had difficulty hearing French accents from the public address system.

Strategically placed electronic advertisements endorsing well-known jewelry, cosmetics, and apparel brands in easy-to-read messages peppered the well-lit terminal. They complimented meticulously clean and bright-colored concessions and created an instant awareness of their availability to potential customers. Mannequins wearing expensive jewelry and colorful clothing communicated, "Here I am, buy what I'm wearing, and you, too, will be as beautiful as I." Additionally, clear, and uncluttered destination signs reflected on super shiny, clean floors. I could have looked up my pant leg for an unobstructed view of my calves and the exquisite tone only years of sitting behind a computer could have helped to develop. Sitting areas with comfortable chairs and bright-colored carpets invited weary passengers to relax.

It seemed our walk through the terminal was longer than the runway our plane used for landing! However, glass formed part of the arch-like ceiling and sidewalls, thus enabling travelers to appreciate and enjoy the natural light that would later peek through the glass design and stimulate the feeling of openness in a large, contained area. I liked this concept because I've been in terminals with monotonous interior design, such as low-hanging ceilings, narrow walkways, dim lighting, and dark-painted walls. Because of these dungeon-like terminals, I anxiously awaited my escape to the outside environment. Breathing polluted air amid congested traffic and loud noises in an unfamiliar city was a refreshing change.

Moving through the airport, I greeted Christina, a young lady walking next to us. As she neared me, I said, "hello." She at once made eye contact and smiled at the three of us. Interestingly, she was originally from Paris, but now worked in Bermuda's hospitality industry. She seemed jubilant and looked forward to visiting her family for the Christmas holidays. Later that evening, I realized a peaceful, polite chat fostered a gift of kindness and civility. What a fantastic welcome to Paris!

After going through customs and retrieving our luggage, we followed a walkway to the regional express train terminal. Along the way, we passed shops, restaurants, lounges, and business facilities and bought train tickets to downtown Paris. Before the trip, we figured a train ride would be exciting and economical. However, as we arrived at the station, the vibration from the train just leaving was quite noticeable. Because it was only six o'clock in the morning, the platform didn't have an ocean of passengers waiting for the next silvery, shiny capsule to arrive as it would have on a typical workday. Instead, electronic destination signs and advertisements sprinkled the spotless, tidy platform. Claudia and I nostalgically reminded each other of the subway rides to Manhattan Island in New York City, where we worked early in our marriage. The public announcement system, train whistles, thunderous engines, and metal wheels screeching to a halt reminded us of younger years.

The inside of our rail car was nearly empty. As I looked around, I noticed a couple embracing and kissing, a young man playing video games, a person napping, and another busily interacting with his cell phone. The ride from the terminal to downtown Paris took approximately 45 minutes. Riding on the train, we saw darkened, wet streets as residential, commercial, and industrial structures reflected upon them. Residences consisted of single and multi-family dwellings and tall apartment buildings. People walking the streets shielded themselves with scarves, heavy coats, and hats from the cold, blistery temperature. Passing hundreds of residences, I wondered about the life stories of those living there and the commonalities they shared with neighbors.

Upon exiting our train in downtown Paris at 7 a.m., the city welcomed us with a cold, drizzly, foggy morning as the black, wet streets mirrored traffic signals and streetlamps. The outside world seemed deserted and like a western ghost town without tumbleweed. Abandoned streets with fog-covered historic buildings, restaurants, and stores added an eerie feeling. As we passed a small park, I imagined zombies coming out to eat us. But happily, McDonald's golden arches shone through the dark desolation and furnished a landmark to determine our location. We then referred to our written directions and quickly reached our home for the next two nights.

Our travel agent at AAA had arranged our stay at a Best Western Hotel on nine rue du 22 Sommerand Street, about a ten-minute walk from the rail station. Its neatness, quaintness, and boutique-style immediately charmed us. The reception clerk was extremely friendly and laughed at my jokes, unlike sleepy-eyed Claudia and Lindsey, who heard similar corny stuff on other occasions. Our eyes widened when told our room on the third floor was available. We made two trips to our oasis because the antique elevator was quite small. Claudia, Lindsey, and their luggage went up first; my suitcase and I went second. As I traveled inside the metal box for the first time, I quickly assured myself the system of metal cables, pulleys, and vertical guide bars would ensure our safety. The elevator's vintage doors cast in gold reminded me of a birdcage. Unlike a pet bird, however, I would soon be free. Thinking back, I already was intensely aware of my surroundings and had begun practicing mindfulness.

Upon entering our room, I quickly noticed its compactness. Initially, I thought it was more suitable for Middle Earth hobbits than for us. On a good day, it may have been able to accommodate six and a half hobbits or maybe eight to ten gremlins with ample dancing space, but insufficient room for an orchestra. However, I was impressed with our temporary abode and how it was well-appointed with the elegant simplicity of the red-painted room, curtains, contemporary furniture, and an unobstructed view of a side street.

After unpacking a few items, we took a short rest. After all, we'd been up for over 20 hours. Fortunately, the crying baby from our flight wouldn't prevent us from enjoying a well-deserved snooze. It was 9 a.m. as we quickly succumbed to the darkness of Middle Earth. Boy, did I feel good! I just laid there with outstretched arms and legs as my giant watermelon head rested on a nice, fluffy pillow welcoming my presence and catering to my quest for relaxation. However, after 20 or so minutes, I discovered I couldn't sleep anymore. After all, we were amid the famous Latin Quarter of Paris! As Claudia and Lindsey slept, I entered a very tight bathroom, climbed over the washbasin, and into the shower stall. A hot shower soothed my senses. I then dressed, grabbed my camera case, and proceeded downstairs to the hotel lobby.

As I walked out of my birdcage, I soon discovered what seemed like a mirage. It was a coffee maker with various kinds of coffee. Oh, my goodness, liquid black gold for just $1.50! After just one sip, I felt a special reverence for a steamy, full-bodied, creamy cup of cheer as my taste buds danced in merriment. I even thought of writing thank you notes to the people responsible for providing this cup of ambrosia to me.

Oohing and aahing over my cup of heavenly bliss, I sat on a contemporary, fashionable sofa in the lobby to reacquaint myself with my camera. However, after several sips of my liquid cheer, I realized I left my charger back home. I started to get mad at myself, but quickly decided to let it go. After all, I still carried my cell phone camera, which took excellent, clear pictures. Soon realizing I could buy a charger, if needed, issues associated with work, project deadlines, and everyday challenges were evaporating into thin air. Instead, I was enjoying the present. In an improved state of mindfulness, I reveled in my coffee, valued the Christmas decorations in the lobby, and delighted in being alone with my thoughts. The beginning of a transformed state of mind was empowering.

Relaxing in a peaceful, heavenly bliss, I briefly interacted with a couple from Madrid, Spain. As I spoke to them in Spanish, my native tongue, I learned they visit Paris during the Christmas Season. Our hand gestures, eye contact, proximity to each other, and smiles revealed trust and willingness to engage in peaceful conversation. The wife's eyes at once grew wide as I mentioned having relatives in Majorca, an island off Spain's coast. In addition to having a dear friend living there, the isle is one of her favorite places. All aspects of our verbal and nonverbal communication and our familiarity with Majorca and other parts of Spain led to a group hug as their airport shuttle arrived. I'd forgotten how it's part of Spanish culture to embrace strangers and non-strangers alike, even if people have just met. I was thankful for the fleeting time we spent together. It was as if we knew each other for years.

After their departure, I went back to the room to gently wake my two sleepy hobbits, who then freshened up, so we could venture out in a city of rich history and beauty. Then, as Claudia and Lindsey prepared themselves, I went back downstairs for another cup of liquid black gold.

Le Jardin du Luxembourg, Latin Quarter, and Musée d'Orsay

After Claudia and Lindsey came downstairs, we stepped out into the streets of the Latin Quarter, located on the West Bank of the Seine River. The Quarter is abundant in history and filled with university students, artists, tourists, restaurants, bars, cultural activities, entertainment, and beautiful architecture. The Paris-Sorbonne University is situated here, along with the Pantheon, Musée Curie, Shakespeare and Company Bookshop, and other well-known historic buildings.

The Le Jardin du Luxembourg and its well-manicured gardens, lawns, flowerbeds, and the historic Medici Fountain, commissioned in the 1600s by Marie de' Medici, widow of Henry IV, was close to our hotel and the Latin Quarter. Trees and well-manicured shrubs reflected on a beautiful pool of water leading to the fountain. Even on a winter day, warmly clothed children rejoiced and enjoyed running on the tree-lined promenade. I imagined how beautiful it must be in spring and summer with different varieties and colors of flowers adorning the landscape. Monuments and statues added to the beauty of the historic gardens.

As we went through the Latin Quarter, we headed toward the Orsay Museum, or Musée d'Orsay. Walking there, I saluted the Latin Quarter's authenticity, history, and people in cafes. In addition, we were walking the very streets and passing restaurants Ernest Hemingway, Victor Hugo, Pablo Picasso, F. Scott Fitzgerald, and other notable figures frequented. Having a background in History and English, this reality exuberated me. I wondered how I would have felt if I'd met these famous individuals. How would I have interacted with them? Conversing with Hemingway may have led to a better understanding of his passion for writing, travel, and participation in some of history's tragic periods, such as World War I and the Spanish Civil War in the 1930s. Although learning about his life through biographies and other sources intrigues me, I would have liked to see his expressions, gestures, and other body movements as he explained what he learned about himself in the challenges, he undertook. Connecting with another individual face-to-face supplies opportunities to learn about myself and find ways to enrich empathy and respect toward others.

We arrived at the Musée d'Orsay after a 45-minute walk through the Latin Quarter and alongside the Seine River's West Bank. It was a bright, sunny afternoon and not very cold. Upon entering, I noticed bright-colored canvases popping off the walls, generously inviting us into the minds and imagination of their creators.

The Musée d'Orsay sits on the left bank of the Seine River.
It was established in 1986. Originally a railway station.

Interestingly, the Orsay houses the most extensive collection of impressionist and post-impressionist artworks by Monet, Cezanne, Van Gogh, Degas, Renoir, and other noted artists. I even took pictures of famous works, such as Van Gogh's *Starry Night over the Rhone*. The painting has intrigued me for years because of how the night sky, stars, and lights reflect on France's Rhone River. Even though I couldn't touch the painting, I could reach out to it and connect with Van Gogh and his creative genius. This reminded me of the Latin Quarter, where my footprints touched the exact steps of renowned writers and artists.

Inside View of Musée d' Orsay

Visiting the museum, I noticed elementary school children intently listening to their teacher as she explained a piece of art. I instantly appreciated a wonderful learning encounter; young students were acquiring art appreciation early in life. In addition, art promotes creativity and critical thinking. When teaching elementary school children, I asked them why they used specific colors, paint strokes, and patterns as they painted scenes. Explaining their reasoning planted the seeds for developing creative and critical thinking skills in later grades. Former colleagues used paintings to promote critical thinking. For instance, they asked their students what they thought about a picture. One of my former colleagues even used Van Gogh's *Starry Night over the Rhone* in her lessons.

Future art scholars!

After visiting the Orsay, we walked alongside the West Bank of the Seine River toward Notre Dame Cathedral. Since pre-medieval times, the river has played a vital role in Paris' history. For example, during the 1900 Summer Olympics, rowing, swimming, and water polo occurred here. During World War II, the First Canadian Army cut off the German 7th Army on the West Bank in the Battle of Normandy.

The Seine River flows through the heart of Paris to the English Channel. It's approximately 485 miles long.

Beautiful bridges join the East and West Banks of the Seine and provide picturesque photo ops. In 1991, the United Nations Educational, Scientific, and Cultural Organization (UNESCO) named the riverbanks a World Heritage Site. Thirty-seven bridges connect both banks; some are monuments unto themselves because of their exquisite designs. Claudia, Lindsey, and I especially enjoyed the Pont Alexandre III bridge, which Parisians consider the most beautiful. Gorgeous bronze candelabras, cherubs, and nymphs embellish the bridge.

Gazing at the Seine River at night, street and other light sources enhanced its beauty and reminded me of lighting's prominence in Van Gogh's *Starry Night over the Rhone*. I admired the bridges' splendor and their reflection off the Seine's dark, chilly water. In addition to its beauty, the river reminded me that it's a thriving waterway, connecting people from all levels of society and worldwide through commerce, sightseeing cruises, and other forms of human interaction.

Claudia and Lindsey on a bridge overlooking the Seine River

Notre Dame Cathedral

Our Lady of Paris, a world-famous example of French Gothic architecture built during the medieval period is located on the Seine's East Bank. Approaching the main entrance on the western facade, there was a short wait to enter the Catholic Cathedral. Interestingly, we stood in the same area where hundreds of people cheered at the end of World War II.

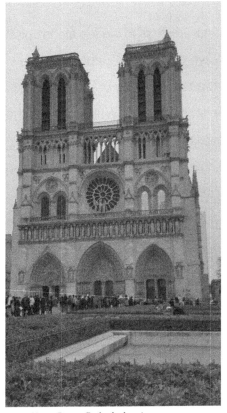

Notre Dame Cathedral main entrance

While waiting, I studied the Cathedral's famed wooden spire, flying buttresses, sculptures, and stained-glass windows. I remember how Claudia, Lindsey, and I enjoyed looking at the facade, containing the Portal of the Virgin, Portal of the Last Judgment, and Portal of St. Anne. I even used my cell phone camera to zoom in on the Tympanum of the Last Judgment and the West Rose Window to study their intricate detail. Immediately above the portals are statues of Israel's kings and two soaring, decorative towers reaching toward the sky overlooking Paris and its watery highway. As Biblical figures and scenes accentuate Notre Dame, Gargoyle statues prominently loom over Paris and visitors to the Cathedral. Admiring the Cathedral's facade, I remembered how Victor Hugo made the South Tower famous through his character, Quasimodo, in *The Hunchback of Notre Dame.*

Visitors climbing almost four hundred steps to the top along spiral stairways can enjoy Paris's renowned bell and panoramic view. Unfortunately, we didn't climb to the top because of hunger pangs. However, we did marvel at Notre Dame's interior. Walking inside the Cathedral was like wandering inside a museum covered with priceless works of art and statues. Three stained-glass rose windows are unique features within the Cathedral. New Testament figures surround Mary in the North Rose Window as the South Rose Window shows Christ surrounded by angels and saints. Other stained-glass windows highlight the Cathedral's beauty.

Additionally, paintings, such as "Saint Thomas Aquinas, Fountain of Wisdom" and "The Visitation," which date back centuries, stood out. The famous Great Organ continues to complement worship. Ten bells, each weighing up to four tons, are housed in the Cathedral as well.

Notre Dame Cathedral interior

Scholars believe three items associated with Jesus are stored in the Cathedral: The Crown of Thorns, pieces of the cross, and a nail that penetrated one of his hands as he hung on the cross. These relics are periodically displayed. Furthermore, relics of the two patron saints of Paris, Saints Denis, and Genevieve, are in the spire.

The Christmas decorations were unquestionably eye-catching. Claudia, Lindsey, and I especially enjoyed a replica of a small village adorned with Christmas decorations. The town reminded me of how local Parisians and tourists visiting the Cathedral were unified in a season "to be born, to plant and reap, to heal, and to laugh." Despite distinct cultural backgrounds, people shared peaceful and joyful emotions during a season symbolizing love and unity among strangers, friends, and families.

Sadly, I learned Notre Dame Cathedral suffered a dreadful fire on April 15, 2019. The blaze collapsed the timber spire and two-thirds of the wooden roof; however, the two bell towers survived the travesty. In addition, because the Cathedral was undergoing renovation, famous artwork was stored throughout Paris. Fortunately, the altar and crucifix stand unharmed as the Cathedral's reconstruction plans are underway. This travesty illustrates the importance of living in the present; the Cathedral captured my undivided attention. Today, I remember my visit as if it were yesterday; should I forget any part of it, my journal reminds me of the joy I still remember.

After completing our visit, we walked across the street and dined at a French restaurant. Before the trip, I didn't consider myself a "foodie," although my wife and daughter were. However, the tastiness of the various dishes we consumed during our trip may have helped transform my appetite for delicious food. Unlike Robert Frost's poem "The Road Not Taken," I like the road I'm currently taking when it comes to joining my taste buds in a dance of succulent merriment. For our first Parisian supper, I graciously devoured French onion soup with cheese oozing down the bowl, and clearly, the best I ever tasted (and in Paris, too! Who would have guessed?). Claudia and Lindsey shared a nicely browned buttery chicken with potatoes and a creamy dessert. The small piece they allowed me to taste was enormously delicious!

During dinner, we chatted about the flight and the day's events. Of course, there was laughing and smiling. Meals often provide us with the opportunity to relish bonding and togetherness. Closeness enables us to trust each other unequivocally and to rely on each other unconditionally.

Dining with Claudia and Lindsey often reminds me of *Field of Dreams* (1989). Being an avid baseball fan, this is one of my favorite movies. Its storyline highlights the dedication and passion fans have for the game. In one part of the film, the main character, Ray Kinsella, asks his father, "Hey…Dad? You wanna have a catch?" The father, John Kinsella, responds, "I'd like that." A game of catch between a father and son, or daughter, denotes a special bond between parent and child. For me, meals with Claudia and Lindsey are like these games of catch.

Shakespeare and Company Bookstore

After a delightful dinner, we walked to the West Bank and took pictures of lights emanating from Notre Dame Cathedral and reflecting on the Seine River. Parts of the Cathedral's western facade reflected beautifully on the water as the wintry night air tried to sneak through our coats and freeze us in time. As the majesty of Notre Dame sparkled on the Seine, we soon reached the famous Shakespeare and Company Bookstore and could still see the Cathedral from a distance. Opened in 1951, the bookstore sells new and used books and serves as a reading library to the public. It provides accommo-

dations to aspiring writers and artists. The store's way of conducting business and building community among interested individuals are genuinely fascinating.

We spent about an hour and a half admiring the store and its thousands of books. Lindsey was like a small child in a candy store. Well, we all were because of our passion for reading. Claudia and I contributed to Lindsey's love for reading after enrolling her in a summer reading club in her middle school years. She

Claudia and I in front of the entrance

soon became an avid reader, which has been a blessing to her. To my surprise, she remembers the thousands of books she's read. On the other hand, I'm fortunate to remember what I read the night before, assuming I don't fall asleep after reading just a few lines.

The original Shakespeare and Company Bookstore opened in the 1920s at a different location, not far from its present one. The shop, a cultural hub from the 1920s to the early 1940s, was a lending library and post office where American ex-pats received their mail. Ernest Hemingway, Gertrude Stein, James Joyce, F. Scott Fitzgerald, and other eminent writers frequented the establishment. Unfortunately, the bookstore closed in 1941 during the German occupation of Paris. Like in many parts of our travel, Claudia, Lindsey, and I visited a place filled with history, making us value our travel even more.

After leaving the bookstore, we walked through the Latin Quarter and passed shops and restaurants adorned with Christmas decorations. The food connoisseurs of our dynamic trio were already making plans for where to eat the next night. After we arrived back at our hotel room, it didn't take long to fall asleep. However, right before engaging in a well-deserved slumber, I remembered how I dozed off in our welcoming bed earlier and rested for only 20 minutes. This time, eight hours of sleep blessed me; the other two hobbits slept another hour.

Day 3 (Monday)

Early in the morning, I made entries in my travel journal as Claudia and Lindsey lingered in their uninterrupted splendor of sleep. I wrote how travel offers people an opportunity to find common ground regardless of race, sex, ethnicity, religion, and other differences. The Musée d'Orsay, Notre Dame Cathedral, and Shakespeare and Company Bookstore provide meeting places for thousands of strangers with similar desires, for example, admiring famous paintings and sculptures and perusing interesting books. As mentioned earlier, I journaled about the worth of being mindful, which began the onset of the harmonious trio.

Louvre Museum

After the sleepyheads awakened, they decided to have breakfast at the hotel to ensure being punctual for our visit to the Louvre Museum, or Musée du Louvre. The European-style breakfast was quite tasty and healthy. Claudia and Lindsey selected assorted items from what appeared to be a traditional French breakfast buffet: cereals, bread, butter, jelly, croissants, pastries, ham, cheese, coffee, and juice. I only drank coffee. Well, I did eat a tiny morsel of Claudia's buttery, warm, flaky croissant. After breakfast, we reviewed our itinerary for the day, which consisted of visiting the Louvre Museum, Avenue des Champs -Élysées-, Arch of Triumph, and the Eiffel Tower.

Heading toward the Louvre, I continued to prize Paris' buildings. From what I've read, the City of Lights is the birthplace of Gothic-style architecture; structures from the Middle Ages to the 21st century dot the city's landscape. Once again, we crossed the Seine to the East Bank. Like the previous evening, I thought about how the Seine is genuinely worthy of reflection.

After about a 30-minute walk, we arrived at the Louvre around 8:30. There was already a line of fellow visitors waiting to enjoy the museum's famous holdings. However, we only waited about 30 minutes before entering the Louvre Pyramid, the main entrance, constructed of glass and metal. Since its completion in 1989, the Pyramid has become a significant landmark. However, controversy surrounds the structure; some argue its modernity doesn't match the Louvre's authentic architecture.

The Louvre, located in the Louvre Palace, was built as a fortress in the 12th century. The museum opened in 1793. There are eight divisions or sections to the museum: Egyptian Antiquities; Near Eastern Antiquities; Greek, Etruscan, & Roman Antiquities; Islamic Art; Sculpture; Decorative Arts; Paintings; Prints and Drawings.

Once inside, we were impressed with the museum's imposing hall-ways decorated with sculptures and paintings from different countries and historical periods. Approximately 38,000 objects from prehistoric to modern-day inhabit the museum's nearly 783,000 square feet. We treasured works during our visit, like the *Venus de Milo*, an ancient Greek marble statue. According to art scholars, the ancient statue influenced later generations, such as Salvador Dali and his celebrated 1936 plaster reproduction of *Venus de Milo with Drawers.*

Louvre Pyramid

Leonardo da Vinci's masterpiece, *Mona Lisa,* draws large crowds of onlookers. A bulletproof, climate-controlled glass case encloses the painting. On the day of our visit, hundreds of onlookers with cameras hovering over their heads took pictures of a world-renowned painting. Lindsey and I sneaked to the front and also took pictures. Initially, she wasn't extremely interested in viewing the portrait because she often saw it in books. However, her eyes widened nearing it. Viewing it in person was truly remarkable! Indeed, we both admired the creative genius of Leonardo da Vinci.

We also marveled at *The Winged Victory of Samothrace*, a second-century marble Hellenistic sculpture honoring the goddess Nike. Climbing an elaborate, long staircase leading to the statue, I noticed the walls' pleasing symmetry and how the ceiling softly blended into the stairway, peering up toward the sky through round skylights.

Our visit to the Louvre was a significant highlight of our trip. However, just enjoying the design of the interior walls, marble floors, ceilings, and windows would have made the visit memorable. Decorative and strategically placed windows enriched photographing the Louvre's architectural splendor. Visitors could easily spend weeks enjoying a magnificent structure and its historical contents.

Avenue des Champs-Élysées

After leaving the Louvre, we walked toward the Arch of Triumph, or Arc de Triomphe, via the famous Avenue des Champs-Élysées. We passed by theatres, restaurants, cafes, luxury clothing stores, and jewelry establishments heading toward the iconic structure. Strolling on the Avenue des Champs-Élysées reminded me of Fifth Avenue in New York City. However, the Champs-Élysées is much broader and lined with trees.

> *The Avenue des Champs-Élysées, one of the most famous streets globally, is a little over a mile long and about 230 feet wide. It's here that the Bastille Day parade is held every year on July 14. Bastille Day commemorates the Bastille attack, which was a turning point of the French Revolution in 1789. The finish for the Tour de France bicycle race is here as well.*

Atrch of Triumph, or Arc de Triomphe

The well-known Arch highlights the Avenue des Champs-Élysées. Claudia and I first visited the Arch in 1975. After joining me for my two-year Army tour in Germany on Christmas Day, I surprised her with a trip to Paris days later. The trip was my Christmas present to her. I gave her a sweater the following year.

The French Emperor, Napoleon, ordered construction of the Arch in 1806. Construction stopped because of Napoleon's abdication. As a result, it was completed in 1836.

As Claudia and I admired the Arch during our first visit, I recalled a renowned picture of Paris' liberation in 1944 and marchers carrying the French and American flags. Crossing the same street depicted in the photo and our footsteps touching the same ground, I felt linked with a historic moment. Although stationed in Germany, I was proud of what American soldiers and other allies did in the European Theater during World War II and how I was a part of tradition.

We witnessed the Arch through different lenses because Lindsey was with us on our second visit to Paris. After all, it'd been over forty years since our last visit. We observed what seemed like millions of cars going around the Arch upon reaching it. It was like seeing the Daytona 500. Fortunately, there's an underground walkway from the Avenue des Champs – Élysées to the bottom of the Arch, making for an easier and safer crossing. Upon reaching its base, Claudia, Lindsey, and I climbed a set of stairs to admire this beautiful landmark. Walking about the Arch, I marveled at its design, prominent location within the city, and historical significance.

The dynamic trio in front of the Arch

Inside the monument are inscriptions of the names of significant battles of the Napoleonic Wars. The names of 558 French generals who fought or died in battles are also listed. The Tomb of the Unknown Soldier from World War I is below the Arch. On November 11 of every year, a ceremony commemorates the signing of an armistice between France and Germany in 1918. As a student, I remember studying world-famous victory marches passing through the Arch, for instance, the Germans in 1871 and 1940. The French and allied forces marched through in 1944 and 1945 to celebrate liberation from German occupation.

Reading the battles' names, I commemorated the individuals who fought and died in these struggles. I wondered what they thought and felt as they marched toward potential death. Moreover, I pondered how mothers, fathers, sisters, brothers, and children were affected by losing a loved one. Did a part of them die as well? Considering these questions, I reminded myself I could continue to learn about past events and still ground myself in the present. Otherwise, I may find myself living in the past and dwelling on the tragedies that occurred without appreciating what the present offers. By recalling France's German occupation and being immersed in the present, I profoundly respected how significant past events positively impacted the present. The suffering millions faced throughout the Second World War reminded me of my desire to increase compassion toward others because of people worldwide suffering the travesty of war and injustice.

Visiting the Arch, I recalled the coordinated November 2015 Paris attacks in Saint-Denis, a northern suburb of Paris. Sadly, three suicide bombers struck outside a stadium during a football match. In addition to committing other atrocities, the attackers took hostages at a concert at the Bataclan Theater. As police raided the place, the attackers either shot or blew themselves up. The attacks resulted in 130 people dying and 350 being wounded. Before leaving on vacation, I finished reading *You Will Not Have My Hate by* Antoine Leirus. He writes about how he lost his wife on November 15 as she attended a concert at the Bataclan Theater. Shortly after losing his wife, Leirus wrote the following open letter to the attackers:

> On Friday night, you stole the life of an exceptional being, the love of my life, the mother of my son, but you will not have my hate. I don't know who you are, and I don't want to know. You are dead souls. You want me scared, to see my fellow citizens through suspicious eyes, to sacrifice my freedom for security. You have failed. I will not change.

Concerning his son, Leirus wrote, "…you will not have his hate either." These sentiments struck a chord in my heart. His words were devoid of the hatred penetrating the world around us for religious and other reasons. The Essenes, an ancient religious sect, addressed Leirus's sentiments particularly well hundreds of years earlier. One of their tenets says, "To heal our world, we begin by becoming the conditions of healing ourselves." Leirus' healing process echoed these words.

Fortunately, a season of kindness and compassion is within our grasp if we reach out to others. For example, merely opening and holding a door for someone at a store, helping a mother load a stroller into her car, and helping an older person carry their groceries are small acts that can significantly affect people. Likewise, volunteering at a homeless shelter or food bank influences the lives of those in need.

Present connecting with the past!

After visiting the Arch, we crossed back to the Avenue des Champs-Élysées and headed toward the Eiffel Tower. Lindsey snapped a picture of Claudia and me across the Arch along the way. It was the exact location where Claudia and I had our photo taken during our 1975 Christmas visit in the "pre-selfie" days. As Lindsey took the picture, I remembered challenges Claudia and I have encountered since our first visit to Paris. Our fondest memories often revolve around travel and the respite it provides. Although we enjoy recollecting pieces of the past, we now make a concerted effort to enjoy the present, which empowers us to better engage in and accept what each day offers.

Eiffel Tower

Continuing toward the Eiffel Tower, we walked through tree-lined residential neighborhoods and small local stores, while viewing the tall icon from a distance.

Gustave Eiffel built the Eiffel Tower for the 1889 Exposition to celebrate the 100th anniversary of the French Revolution. Its completion symbolized a milestone in France's technological achievements in the industrial era. The Tower's height is 1,063 feet, or 324 meters (about the height of an 81-story building).

After reaching our destination at six o'clock, we decided to stop at a local food stand to appease our palates. Oh yes, it was munchie time! Lindsey ate a chocolate-filled crepe oozing with steamy, tasty, creamy chocolate. Claudia and I shared a delicious crepe filled with various kinds of melted cheese. The steam emanating from our crepes warmed us from the brisk evening air. These thin, delicate pancakes of heavenly enjoyment were absolute ecstasy! We enjoyed eating our "creepies," as I like to call them, as we sat on a bench across the Eiffel Tower. Sitting down, even on a frigid evening, was extremely relaxing to our wearied feet.

Indulging in our crepes reminded me of valuing the little things, even if they occurred years before. While savoring our culinary delights, I thought of having breakfast with my Aunt Asyria and Uncle

Ruben as a young child in the Bronx. For almost two years, my aunt invited me to eat breakfast with them on Sunday mornings. One of her favorite dishes consisted of crepes filled with ham and cheese. These amazing delights were unquestionably delicious and melted in my mouth. Munching on our "creepie" in front of the Eiffel Tower, I found how being reflective at any given moment can result in time travel! As we finished our crepes and walked closer to the Eiffel

Eiffel Tower

Tower, I couldn't help but smile at the memory of Aunt Asyria and Uncle Ruben and the love they shared with me. The noise of moving traffic did not prevent me from reminiscing; in fact, I didn't even hear it. I chalked this up to being mindfully immersed in and content with the moment.

It was around six-thirty in the evening as the day began turning into night. The sparkling lights of the Eiffel Tower beautifully illuminated the evening with golden splendor and loomed over the surrounding area sprinkled with thousands of admirers. In addition, the multicolored lights emanating from the Tower brilliantly reflected on the Seine River. Although we didn't climb to the top, I noticed what seemed to be specks of people partaking in a panoramic view from the Tower's observation deck. Looking up, I wondered what thoughts and feelings were permeating through their minds. Were they focused on the lights and their beautiful reflection on the Seine River, or were they thinking of how crowded the streets were and what they would eat later in the evening? If I'd been on the observation deck, what would I have thought about? Would I have been reflective, or would I have thought of getting up early the following day? However, being on the ground, I was especially appreciative of the cold, brisk air and how the Tower's lights reflected on the water.

As it got darker, I took pictures of the well-lighted Eiffel Tower. After enjoying its grandeur from a close-up view, we walked back toward the Latin Quarter alongside the Seine. We occasionally stopped to enjoy the Tower's view from a distance and rest our aching feet.

After all, we probably walked about ten miles if we included our visit to the Louvre's subterranean labyrinths. Lamenting over our tired, touristy feet, I noticed families asking for food and money, which reminded me of the homeless population in the U.S. and other parts of the world. I have often thought of how to better alleviate the situation, in addition to donating time and money to charitable organizations.

Saveurs de Savoie: Home to fine French dining!

Finally, we arrived at the Latin Quarter and ate at another French Restaurant. Again, Claudia and Lindsey shared a meal. They delighted themselves with cheese fondue, masterfully dipping the savory bread into the thick, luscious, melted cheese. I embraced another flavorful, pleasing French Onion soup. Enjoying our supper, I fondly recalled the first fondue Claudia and I shared in Zermatt, Switzerland, when visiting in the 1970s. It was so delicious that, to this day, a heavenly cheesy delight is still one of our favorite dishes. Who knew the simplicity of blending several types of cheese and wine could cause such culinary ecstasy? I remember hitting my head on an overhead lamp as we got up to leave the restaurant; fortunately, the pain has long since subsided. Moments like these are an oasis in times of turmoil and engender deep gratitude for the ups and downs we've shared in our marriage.

After our night of fine French cuisine, we headed back to the hotel and prepared for our journey to Germany the next day. As my two Middle Earth hobbits packed and readied for a good night's sleep, I wrote about our visits to the Louvre and Orsay, focusing on how artists' sculptures and paintings conveyed their imagination and desire to connect with their audience. Was it merely a way to express a unique talent? Why did they communicate what they did in the way they did? Why did they use specific color schemes, brush strokes, and line patterns? In addition, I realized several artists' paintings showed their grief over atrocities occurring during their lifetime. For instance, in Shakespeare and Company, I read how Picasso used one of his most famous paintings, *Guernica*, to voice his anguish over the killing of innocent women and children during the Spanish Civil War. (In 1937, Nazi and Italian airplanes indiscriminately bombed the Spanish city of Guernica.).

I also recalled how the Latin Quarter's streets embraced the imprints of writers, such as Hemingway, Hugo, Fitzgerald, and others. In *A Moveable Feast*, I remembered how Hemingway wrote about his struggles as a young expatriate journalist and writer in Paris during the 1920s. After reading the book in college, I empathized with what

Hemingway went through since Claudia and I often struggled financially and were uncertain about our financial future. Walking the same streets, I shared with his struggles as a young writer and journalist even though I underwent different challenges. This made the Latin Quarter come alive! It's astounding distinguished writers and artists continue to attract the respect and admiration of millions worldwide.

Grand monuments, like the Arch, are reminders of violence and past conflicts between and within nations. Yet, invariably, they invigorate and water the seeds of being thankful for past generations' sacrifices and whose successes we enjoy today. Although I served in the military, I never saw the bloodshed and travesty of battle and loss of human life in combat. However, I formed a relationship with soldiers that endured the horrors of war in Vietnam. Some suffered posttraumatic stress disorder and wore the travesty of war in their sullen, sunken eyes. It seemed a part of them died in the war. A colleague of mine in Germany served in Vietnam and experienced enemy attacks. Because of these incidents, he encountered recurring nightmares. However, we bonded through laughter and the challenges of facing everyday military life, such as being separated from loved ones in month-long field exercises. I remember seeing a combat veteran's joy and happiness as he greeted his long-awaited daughter into the world. Like me, many of my Army buddies grew up in neighborhoods ravished with violence. The inscriptions in the Arch of Triumph and memories of visiting the Vietnam Memorial, Korean Memorial, and the World War I and II Memorials in Washington, D.C., reminded me of how we're all interrelated through life's challenges, including joyful events and tribulations.

In our visit to Paris, we saw the "darlings" of the city and how poverty, hunger, and homelessness constitute vital issues worldwide. Since returning to the U.S., we've increased our contributions, time, and other resources to help those in need in Tallahassee and around the world, regardless of cultural and other differences. This mindset enables me to be thankful for helping and serving others while simultaneously being grateful for the blessings in my life. A loving family, a beautiful, modest home, ample food to eat, a comfortable bed, pillows (I like lots of pillows), spending time with Claudia and Lindsey, and the ability to transform my thoughts into words are precious gifts.

AU REVOIR PARIS!

Chapter 4

Deutschland and Österreich

Day 4 (Tuesday)

Flying to Munich, or München, I fondly remembered when Claudia and I lived in Germany during my two-year U.S. Army assignment. We traveled throughout Germany, France, Switzerland, Austria, and Italy throughout this period, enjoying the people, culture, scenic beauty, and food, especially bratwursts and schnitzel. We especially relished how Germany's quaint villages dotted the countryside. In fact, we lived in a small town, Bergrheinfeld, a 15-minute drive from my base.

I enlisted in the U.S. Army from 1975 to 1978. Most of my tour was with the 3rd Infantry Division in Schweinfurt, just north of Wurzburg, in Bavaria. I was so fortunate Claudia accompanied me!

The Josef Strauss Munich International Airport, the second busiest in Germany, provided a gateway to our visit. It led to what this remarkable city offered regarding its people, beauty, history, architecture, and museums. Claudia and Lindsey also anticipated these things and looked forward to interacting with residents and tourists alike. Smelling authentic German food in vendor stands and hearing German voices over loudspeakers reminded me of when Claudia and I lived in Germany. Throughout the terminal comfortable seating arrangements, brightened by natural and interior lighting, enriched our journey as images of travelers reflected on shiny, checkered floors. Signs to the departure gates had bright blue backgrounds and bold white lettering; even I could read them without wearing my glasses. The Munich Airport Center connects the airport's two terminals, sprinkled with shops, restaurants, business facilities, and other amenities. A tent-like glass ceiling enclosed the Center and allowed the sun to peek in and cast shadows over the interior. One of the electric rapid rail systems called the S-Bahn, reminded me of Charles de Gaulle International Airport and its proximity to an adjoining train stop. We didn't go through customs since Germany is a member of the European Union.

As of this writing, approximately 1.5 million people live in Munich, the capital of Bavaria. This makes it the third largest city in Germany after Berlin and Hamburg. An additional six million people live in the Munich metropolitan area.

From the airport, we went on a 45-minute bus ride to downtown Munich, our hotel's location. The Marriott Courtyard, on Schwanthalerstrasse 3, welcomed us with open arms. Situated in Munich's central part, it's close to major attractions, including Karlsplatz, the hub for the electric rail rapid systems called the S-Bahn and U-Bahn. The hotel clerk was exceptionally friendly and eagerly assigned our room. Unlike our small quarters in Paris, the room was modern and spacious with a main street view. There was room to accommodate dozens of hobbits, gremlins, and a small orchestra. Those wishing to dance would have had ample space!

After unpacking and freshening up, we explored the hotel. The lobby was small but comfortable, with people relaxing and using free Wi-Fi. People from different countries enriched the lobby's atmosphere. This diversity reminded me of Munich's population and its foreign nationals: Turks, Albanians, Croats, Serbs, Greeks, Austrians, Italians, and its German population. We also scoped out where we would partake in a daily breakfast buffet extravaganza. Finally, we reviewed our itinerary before leaving the hotel; it included enjoying Marienplatz, the Church of Saint Michael's, the New City Hall, and the Hofbräuhaus.

Marienplatz

Upon leaving the hotel, I bought cold medicine for Lindsey. Interestingly, it cost around seven dollars. Since the same brand and size cost $19 in the U.S. I became disturbed by the price difference. However, upon leaving the store, and as we walked toward Marienplatz, I reminded myself to enjoy the present, and my displeasure over the price difference soon disappeared.

Marienplatz is a pedestrian-only zone peppered with shops, restaurants, historical places, and churches. During the Middle Ages, this city center had ample space for markets and tournaments. Currently, the Christmas Market, or Christkindlmarkt, is held here. These markets are famous throughout Germany in the holiday season. Strolling on Marienplatz's long, wide streets, I remembered studying the plaza's history and learning how parts of the city were severely damaged because of allied bombing in World War II and later rebuilt through the collaboration of thousands of individuals. I'm sure residents of war-torn Munich and surrounding areas appreciated this cooperation and respected others' labor and commitment to rebuilding the city.

Marienplatz is in Munich's city center. It has been Munich's main square since 1158.

While enjoying Munich's Christmas Market, I remembered visiting Nuremberg's Christkindlmarkt in December 1975 before Claudia joined me from the U.S. As I walked and partook in the delightful scents of baked bread, bratwursts, and other edible delights, an older German gentleman walked up to me and spit on my face. Rather than confronting him, I walked on in puzzlement. As I waited for Claudia and Lindsey to join me in the hotel lobby the following day, I wrote about the incident in my journal. Unlike years before, I placed myself in this older man's shoes. I thought he might have gone through undue, horrific hardships, for example, losing loved ones in the course of World War II.

The accuracy or inaccuracy of my reasoning was immaterial. The gentleman saw something about me that caused sadness or bought grave displeasure toward an American (I think my army jacket and closely cropped haircut may have given me away!). His spitting may have exhibited whatever resentment, bitterness, hatred, anger, or grudge he may have held for years. But who was I to judge at the time? Who am I to judge now? Instead, I can empathize with him and endeavor to understand why a fellow human being would succumb to such an act. If I could travel back in time, I would look at the gentleman, smile, and try to shake his hand. Then, I would offer him a hot chocolate, beer, or bratwurst. Maybe all three!

The *Golden Rule* comes to mind: "Do unto others as you would like done unto yourself." If I could revisit the incident, I would make a peaceful gesture of reaching out to someone with kindness and compassion. Possibly, this small act would help reconcile and heal the gentleman's deep-seated issues. It might even prevent him from nourishing other seeds of bitterness and resentment toward others. Even if my actions didn't work, it would be worth trying.

Claudia, Lindsey, and I stopped at food vendor stands to enjoy Christmas trinkets and the smell of popcorn, cotton candy, and bratwursts. The distinctive aroma of popcorn and cotton candy reminded me of visiting the Ringling Brothers Circus with my sister, Miriam, on an Easter Sunday when I was around 11 years old. This was an occasion I'll never forget. Brother and sister spent quality time together and joyously shared a memorable event. Trapeze acts, tightrope walkers, juggling acts, lion tamers, and colorfully clothed clowns with brightly colored faces, among other acts, embellished a special day. Interestingly, the present moment can also include a pleasurable and loving memory!

A view of Marienplatz

In addition to strolling through the Christmas Market, I tried to connect with others. After smiling at passersby, they smiled right back. As we stopped at souvenir and food vendor stands, I often looked at people close to me and pointed to certain items such as Christmas ornaments. I would then look at them, smile, and say "gute," which means "good" in German. These simple interactions created a common bond with strangers in a season of peace.

Church of Saint Michael's

The Jesuit Church of Saint Michael's, the largest Renaissance church north of the Alps, is on Marienplatz. Groundbreaking for this beautiful building began in 1583; it was consecrated in 1597 upon completion. Federico Sustris and Wolfgang Muller began planning this iconic structure in 1582. I especially delighted in its beautifully designed ceiling and decorative, arch-shaped windows. In addition, the altar's gold color contrasted quite nicely with the white colors of the walls, the beige marble floors, and the deep brown pews.

In addition to being an artist, it's my understanding Sustris was a self-taught architect. The fact he was the principal architect for Duke William V of Bavaria stresses having confidence in himself despite his lack of professional training in the field. I appreciated he didn't seem to allow fear or inhibition to thwart his creativity and ability. Consequently, I liked Saint Michael's even more. Like Sustris, I have self-taught myself conflict resolution skills, team building, anger management, and restorative justice. I had the confidence and determination to excel in these areas regardless of formal, professional training, and have delivered hundreds of workshops and seminars on these subjects.

Therefore, I respect and appreciate others who don't let a lack of formal training interfere with what they want to accomplish. Although formal instruction is crucial in some specialties, we can pursue specific areas of interest informally. For example, a former col-

Inside St. Michael's

league is a self-taught artist who moved to North Carolina. Since living there, she has sold hundreds of her works in her adopted state. Fortunately, the harmonious trio doesn't require formal training, only the desire to practice it.

New City Hall

After visiting Saint Michael's, we approached the New City Hall, or Neues Rathaus, constructed from 1867 until 1908 to accommodate a need for additional government offices. The building is the seat of power; it also houses shops and a tourist information center. A Ratskeller, a traditional restaurant serving traditional Bavarian food, is in the basement.

Now, I'm not an architect, but the New City Hall is a splendid piece of neo-gothic architecture. As I admired the building, I thought of how laborers' coordinated efforts ensured the skilled placement of bricks and shell limestone. Glass windows and statues of saints and other figures adorn the main entrance's front façade and would have needed extraordinary diligence in being constructed and sculpted. Beautiful chandeliers, marble floors, large wooden doors, spiral staircases, and vaulted ceilings highlight the building's interior. While walking on the shiny well-laid floors, I thought of the painstaking effort workers in charge of placing the marble must have exercised. I also reflected on the people entrusted with maintaining the building in its current magnificence and helping to ensure visitors, like ourselves, enjoy its splendor.

A Glockenspiel, or clock tower, also sits atop the new city hall. Onlookers enjoy the sounds of delightful chimes as they watch motorized and brightly painted figurines twirl around a newly married King and Queen daily. Also, the colorfully, well-dressed newlyweds enjoy a medieval jousting tournament followed by a ceremonial dance. A cuckoo clock marks the end of each performance, which lasts between 12 to 15 minutes. Because of its popularity, crowds begin

New City Hall and Glockenspiel

gathering below the tower 15 to 20 minutes before each presentation. The enchanted voices of small children marveling at the attraction enhanced my enjoyment of it.

Afterward, we walked toward the Hofbräuhaus, a favorite place for celebrating Oktoberfest, an autumn festival. Along the way, we passed by the Old City Hall, or Altes Rathaus, another beautiful gothic structure. Interestingly, current-day Munich has an eclectic mix of historical and modern architecture. As mentioned earlier, bombing raids destroyed historic buildings during World War II.

While strolling, I overhead a group of people discussing recent killings at a Christmas Market in Berlin. One person had a matter of fact, low rough voice, and commanded others' attention. As the group listened attentively with downcast eyes, one member had direct eye contact with the croaky-voiced individual.

Because I didn't hear the conversation's entirety, I read about the incident the following day. According to the newspaper account, two men deliberately drove a truck into a Christmas market in Berlin, killing twelve people and injuring fifty-six others on December 19, 2016. The driver was found dead in the passenger seat of the truck. Days later, I read where the other perpetrator died in a shootout with police near Milan, Italy. News sources attributed the attack to the Islamic State of Iraq and the Levant (ISIL). Once again, violence reared its ugly, hateful head. What appeared like a joyous, peaceful season was offset by individuals exhibiting violence toward themselves and others.

As we walked through the Marienplatz, I thought about Berlin and the Christmas Market we were thoroughly enjoying. There must have been similarities between both markets; local food scents and aromas must have filled the air and whet visitors' appetites while basking in the holiday season. I asked myself how to transform the violence committed against innocent individuals into increased compassion toward others on Christmas and the upcoming year. How could I help change a narrative often burdened with verbal, emotional, and physical abuse? This memoir and the harmonious trio, in part, are a response to these questions.

Hofbräuhaus

As we headed toward the Hofbräuhaus, we stopped and asked a police officer for directions. The Hofbräuhaus and its massive overhanging chandeliers, wall paintings, and brightly colored vaulted ceiling with images of wine, beer, and rustic country scenes, is a vast Bavarian beer hall with authentic regional food. It's popular among locals and tourists. We found a picnic-style table to our liking after walking through crowded rooms, archways, columns, and sounds of laughter. To our enjoyment, a band of four musicians dressed in lederhosen played oompah music as patrons drank rivers of beer.

Inside view of the Hofbräuhaus

Long tables and benches were reserved for frequent visitors who kept their beer steins on shelves along the walls.

The oompah music embellished a warm, soft pretzel with cheese dip. We then selected from various traditional Bavarian food: veal sausages, weiner sausages with homemade potato salad, baked Bavarian meatloaf, Munich-style sauerbraten, spaetzle egg noodles, and fried sausage with sauerkraut. While sharing some of these Bavarian delights, we reminisced about our trip and the places we wanted to visit in Munich.

Our lunch reminded me of the times Claudia, and I ate regional food during my assignment in Germany. One of our favorite places was a Gasthaus, a German-style inn or tavern, in Grafenrheinfeld, a five-minute car ride from where we lived. Our favorite dish was pork schnitzel with salad and French fries, or pomfrets. The oversized schnitzel often draped over our plates. Although Claudia eats like a bird, she devoured her schnitzel as if she'd been stranded on a desert island for months. We also listened to recent hits, such as those from the band ABBA. Patrons sang along with ABBA as they immersed themselves in conversation, laughter, schnitzel, and beer. As we quietly conversed with each other, we saw others enjoying themselves. To this day, Claudia and I fondly reminisce about the tasty schnitzels we ate here.

As I remember eating at our favorite Gasthaus, I wish we had more diligently engaged with local guests. Living in a small, local community, we could have immersed ourselves in local customs and befriended its residents. Even today, Claudia and I don't know why we didn't avail ourselves of this chance. Maybe we just wanted to share alone time because of my field exercises; these lasted four or more weeks at a time. However, I recall being introverted and shy in my youth and into my twenties. In college, I went to class, studied in the library, completed assignments, and went home. I only socialized with my closest friends and didn't reach out to others. I was content living in my one-way bubble where I could look out, but others couldn't look in.

After my discharge from the Army, attending graduate school opened doors to leave my introverted shell and reach out to teachers and fellow students. Discussing different academic subjects and world events helped me to become more outgoing. Unfortunately, I recognize I did not express gratitude to my teachers and fellow students for helping me to step out of my comfort zone. However, I've also learned to practice self-compassion and, as a result, have forgiven myself for my shortcoming. Fortunately, Claudia and I now reach out to people, thus learning more about ourselves and others. Now, I better understand others' views on diverse topics, thus causing me to reflect on my values and beliefs. Consequently, I've deepened my knowledge and understanding of diverse issues and human behavior, which has impacted my quality of life and happiness. Oh yes, I've increased my thinking skills as well!

As we sat and relaxed in the Hofbräuhaus, Claudia and Lindsey drank soft drinks as I downed both a Helles and a Dunkles beer. A Helles is a traditional German pale lager beer produced mainly in southern Germany. A Dunkles is a dark German beer, ranging from amber to a dark, reddish-brown, and malty flavor. I drank both beers in authentic German liter mugs with "Hofbräuhaus" inscribed on them. In fact, dear friends of ours also gave us a German Beer Stein as a going away gift upon my reassignment to Fort Riley, Kansas, home of the 1st Infantry Division. The stein, situated in a prominent place in our living room, continues to bring back fond memories and plays a joyous German melody.

Famous people have visited the Hofbräuhaus: Thomas Wolfe, Louis Armstrong, Mikhail Gorbachev, and John F. Kennedy. Wolfgang Amadeus Mozart is supposed to have lived nearby as well. On the way back to the hotel, we enjoyed Marienplatz and retired early in the evening. We couldn't resist the lure of oversized soft pillows calling our names.

Day 5: Garmisch-Partenkirchen

Not being present is risky and can prevent meaningfully connecting with another individual. While sitting at a table waiting for Claudia and Lindsey to eat breakfast in the hotel restaurant, I waited fifteen minutes for service and became irritated. As my server approached, he at once apologized and said he had just received a distressing call from his wife. His demeanor awakened me faster than my first cup of coffee. To my chagrin, I unfairly criticized an individual I had never met because I didn't get my coffee promptly. Patience, enjoying families around me, a large breakfast bar, and authentic German music in the background went unnoticed simply because I didn't appreciate what the present offered. Instead, I was distracted by perceived slow service.

Exploring the ski towns of Garmisch-Partenkirchen and Partnach Gorge highlighted the day's itinerary. Fortunately, the train was on time for its eight o'clock departure as only a few travelers boarded. Passing through beautiful snow-covered scenery marked with small villages, churches, and quaint farmhouses made the one-and-a-half-hour ride go quickly.

---

*Garmisch-Partenkirchen is a beautiful
Bavarian alpine village and ski resort situated
in southern Germany and borders Austria.*

Upon arriving at the Garmisch-Partenkirchen train station, we immediately noticed the brightness of the sun's rays and the chilly air; it must have been around 30 degrees Fahrenheit. We walked from the station to the tourist center in the heart of the alpine village. Living in Germany, Claudia and I visited the town occasionally. Painted scenes of Bavaria still adorned the outside walls of residential and commercial buildings. Window boxes with blooming flowers continued to decorate and embellish the buildings' attractiveness.

Painted scenes of Bavarian culture

However, the abundance of tourist stores, restaurants, cafes, and visitors overshadowed the quietude and quaintness Claudia and I enjoyed years before and overwhelmed my fond recollection of the alpine village. Despite these changes, I remembered how the ski resort was an escape from the toils of a highly disciplined military life. Visiting the town during my enlistment enhanced the freedom to enjoy beautiful, breathtaking scenery and engage in outdoor activities, such as bike riding and hiking; this whetted an increased appetite for a civilian lifestyle. Nevertheless, I'm still glad I joined the military because it allowed me to explore it as a potential career choice, honorably serve my country, and travel overseas with Claudia.

Partnach Gorge

We asked for directions upon reaching the tourist center. Since the walking distance to Partnach Gorge was almost four miles, we decided to take public transportation. As we walked to the nearest bus stop, we meandered through the same streets Sherman Tanks of the U.S. 10th Armored Division rolled through in April 1945 after liberating the village. Approaching the bus station, I imagined how residents felt upon liberation from Nazi rule. As a result, I was reminded of victory parades going through the Arch of Triumph and folks being thankful for being freed from tyranny. For a moment, I imagined myself amid inhabitants of Garmisch-Partenkirchen in 1945 and thought of the horrors they witnessed, such as bombing raids, the devastation of homes and neighborhoods, and living under tyranny and oppression. These realities enabled me to empathize with others' hardships and travesties, even if they happened decades ago. Interestingly, past events can kindle compassion for similar present ones. I remember fast-forwarding to the present and the growing concern Claudia,

Lindsey, and I have for those suffering from the brutality happening worldwide.

After boarding the bus, I saw locals doing their daily activities in residential neighborhoods. I especially liked the presence of fellow passengers, such as young children going to their grade school. After a 20-minute bus ride, we arrived at Partnach Gorge, home of the 1936 Winter Olympics skiing events. Being a history nerd, I thought about the games and how the Nazi regime sent fellow human beings to concentration camps as others observed the international competition. Regrettably, horrific acts of inhumanity were happening in Germany and other parts of Europe amid such beautiful, wondrous, snow-covered scenery. Sadly, I thought back to my first visit to Nuremberg, Germany, in the early part of my Army tour in late 1975.

I remember getting up early on a Sunday morning and riding a trolley to Nuremberg Stadium. Upon arrival, I noticed I was the only one there and had a very eerie feeling. I remember feeling overwhelmed after considering what it symbolized. As I looked at the central wall of the stadium, I saw a faded swastika. This sent chills up my spine as I imagined thousands of Nazi Troops marching on stadium grounds. According to historical accounts, the stadium was the site of six Nazi Party rallies from 1933 to 1938. As a college student, I remembered studying about the Nazi Party in Germany and other countries. However, standing in the middle of Nuremberg Stadium and visualizing thousands of Nazi troops marching amid roaring crowds created a sadness I had never felt through reading and writing about the period. Unlike the beautiful scenery surrounding Partnach Gorge, there wasn't any reprieve to my experience at Nuremberg Stadium, only the solace of traveling back to my hotel in downtown Nuremberg. I remember reflecting on the hatred still permeating through the minds of millions.

The early morning visit to Nuremberg Stadium also intensified my desire to study the Holocaust. Consequently, I've read a considerable number of books, in addition to visiting the United States Holocaust Memorial Museum in Washington, DC, the Simon Wiesenthal Center/Museum of Tolerance in Los Angeles, California, and the Florida Holocaust Museum in St. Petersburg. The museums' contents include images of men, women, and children marching to their deaths. Photographs of survivors resembling skeletons after being liberated by allied forces are engraved in my mind. A freight car that carried hundreds of human beings to their death and prominently displayed in the Florida Holocaust Museum in St. Petersburg brought the Holocaust to life. This has had a lasting effect on me. Thankfully, I've found ways to commemorate a sad moment in human history.

During the Second World War, the German Nazi regime was responsible for the mass murder of approximately six million European Jews and members of other groups.

Partnach Gorge captured our senses and cast a spell on us. The Gorge is 2,303 feet long, or approximately 702 meters. In some places, it's 260 feet deep, or about eighty meters. It was about a 25-minute walk from the stadium to the actual Gorge. The stadium also serves as a starting point to hiking trails leading to Mount Zugspitz, the highest mountain in Germany at 9,718 feet. Walking away from the stadium, we noticed a sign for a romantic horse-drawn carriage ride to the Gorge's entry point. Although I offered Lindsey and Claudia the opportunity to ride on the carriage, Lindsey thought it would have been strange for parents and their daughter to go on a romantic carriage ride. She said, "That's just too weird. Let's walk." So, we did.

A scenic view of Partnach Gorge

The Gorge's cottony snow-covered magnificence, frozen water-falls, and trickling icicles overwhelmed us. Tranquil water basins and overhanging cliffs enriched the Gorge, while its serenity and splendor freed us from tumultuous world events and the stress that often plagues us. Moreover, the ice-covered mountainside and crevices provided a gallery of natural beauty embellished with ice and snow formations; their splendor consumed me. As I focused on the scenery and listened to the soothing river sound below, a sense of peace and calmness overtook me. A heightened awareness of the Gorge's grandeur also deepened my connection with nature.

Another gorgeous view of Gorge

Hiking the Gorge wasn't strenuous, and although we could have walked further, we turned back after two miles. Occasionally, we stepped aside to allow others to pass by and vice versa, resulting in smiles and thank-yous. It was about three o'clock when we returned to the stadium and the bus stop. Oh yes, it must have been about 30 degrees Fahrenheit that day.

A view Garmisch-Partenkirchen

Nevertheless, our return bus ride was delightfully warm and cozy. If I'm not mistaken, the students who rode the bus with us in the morning traveled with us again. I wondered if they had enjoyed their day as much as Claudia, Lindsey, and I relished our stay at Partnach Gorge.

Once we got off the bus, we walked around the downtown area of Garmisch-Partenkirchen, including a Christmas Market. As in Munich, the scents of bratwursts and other German staples added to the holiday atmosphere. Soon, we decided to eat at a locally owned, quaint restaurant.

On the train ride back to Munich, we dozed off for part of the trip. The Austrian Alps' fresh mountain air still circulating through our lungs and influencing our drowsiness and tired bodies must have induced such a heavenly bliss! At the hotel, we partook in a round of refreshments in the dining area. Again, it was pleasant to see how patrons approved of their drinks, food, conversations, and sports games on televisions. Finally, after an hour or so, we went upstairs and slept ever so delightfully and peacefully. What a day!

Day 6: Salzburg

While waiting for Claudia and Lindsey to join me for breakfast, I interacted with a heavy smoker in the hotel lobby, which detracted me from attentively listening to his remarks about recent immigration issues in Germany. (Indeed, the countries we visited were experiencing issues like those in the United States). Amid our brief conversation, I learned his mother was seriously injured in a car accident. This contributed to increased smoking and feeling alone and lost. If I'd been on trial for judging his behavior, I would have been found guilty. However, as we continued our discussion, I overcame my negative judgment and replaced my attitude with compassion.

Although I could not resolve my server's challenges from the previous morning and the individual mentioned above, they thanked me for listening. Willingness to ease another's pain is essential for connecting and empathizing with others. Listening to these two individuals' turmoil also showed how active and mindful listening exude compassion toward others. In the course of our conversations and after overcoming my initial negativity toward the two gentlemen, I repeated what they said at critical moments to express interest in their dilemmas. This appeared to stimulate their willingness to interact with me. What a gift so early in the day!

Upon joining me for breakfast, Claudia, Lindsey, and I discussed our bus tour to Salzburg, Austria, which would leave in about two hours. We also consumed another delicious breakfast of regional food consisting of homemade omelets, scrambled eggs, smoked salmon from the North Sea, assorted mouthwatering cheeses, various kinds of bread, and other delicacies. The croissants were fresh, warm, flaky, and delicious. Lindsey had already become quite fond of the restaurant's variety of tea selections. Ah, yes, so much tea, so little time!

After enjoying our meal and welcoming the day, we joined other tourists on our bus tour to Salzburg, the filming location of *The Sound of Music*. As with our trip to Garmisch-Partenkirchen, we passed by spectacular snow-covered countryside with interspersed farms, small villages, and churches. Salzburg's scenic mountains and lakes are incredibly eye-catching and a welcome entrance to the city, known as the "Florence of the North." Vienna, another famous, beautiful city, and Austria's capital is near Salzburg.

Salzburg is the fourth biggest Austrian city and capital of the federal state of Salzburg. At one point in its history, it controlled half of today's Austria.

Upon arrival, our tour group disembarked in the New Town, or Neustadt part of Salzburg, and began a five-hour walking tour. After a short stroll, we arrived at Mirabell Gardens and Palace (site of the "Do-Re-Mi" song from *The Sound of Music)*. A statue of Pegasus,

the winged horse, is prominently placed on the beautifully manicured grounds. The Grand Fountain, with symbols of fire, air, earth,
and water, adorns the landscape as well. Also decorating the estate
are statues of Roman Gods, such as Diana, Flora, Minerva, Venus,
and Hercules. Furthermore, the palace is a showcase of Baroque
architecture. Marble Hall is considered one of Austria's most famous because of its history and highly ornate Baroque style.

Statue of Pegasus, the winged horse

Throughout the year, the works of Wolfgang Amadeus Mozart
(1756-91) enliven the hall with chamber music and orchestra concerts.
Interestingly, Mozart also played at Marble Hall. The annual Salzburg
Festival is held yearly between mid-July to the end of August. Mozart
Week and the Easter Music Festival also bring thousands of people
to the musical mecca of Salzburg. Our visit to Mirabell Gardens and

Palace revealed the appreciation and respect Austrians and others continue to have for music and the arts. People around the world still revere the musical genius of Mozart and other eminent classical composers, such as Haydn, Beethoven, Brahms, and Shubert. The Vienna Boys Choir and Vienna Philharmonic Orchestra are still world-famous.

Since our return, I've read where Mozart traveled to London, Paris, Italy, and Germany to further his understanding of distinctive compositional approaches. I'm sure becoming aware of and listening to different compositional styles included being in the present. Consequently, Mozart's creativity and perspective on musical composition would have been enriched. Similarly, being aware and mindful of the present can significantly influence our approach to and view of everyday life. To me, the Arch of Triumph and the streets of Garmisch-Partenkirchen stimulated a greater awareness and understanding of past generations and their experiences in tumultuous times, such as World War II. Although I wasn't writing a musical score, I began composing a mindset connecting and empathizing with past and present generations. This deepened perspective has increased my compassion for the millions of people experiencing all forms of violence worldwide. Fortunately, non-governmental organizations and religious entities are trying to alleviate national and international violence, including poverty. Happily, promoting oneness and harmony among all people has not been forgotten and lives on.

After visiting Mirabell Gardens and Palace, our tour guide escorted us across the milky green Salzach River; the waterway forms the border between Bavaria and the Austrian states of Salzburg and Upper Austria. I didn't know it at the time, but the winding river, which is 140 miles, or 225 kilometers long, eventually flows into the Danube. The bridge across the Salzach led to the historic Old Town, or Altstadt declared a World Heritage Site in 1996. While sightseeing in the Old Town, we visited Salzburg Cathedral, a city centerpiece; Mozart's birthplace and residence; Mozart Square; Church of Saint Michael;

Saint Peter's Abbey and Cemetery; and Salzburg's oldest bakery. Each site exhibited Salzburg's prominence in history and its fascination with beautiful, ornate, Baroque architecture, in addition to Baroque music and art. The Baroque period began in Rome in the 17th century and spread through Europe and Latin America. After visiting these places, we had three hours to tour independently.

View of Old Town from Salzach River

Being on our own, we admired Old Town's cobbled streets, especially Getreidegassee, the main street. The avenue and its beautifully ornamented stores with wrought iron signs must look the same as in Mozart's time. As we strolled, I thought of how earlier generations benefitted from quaint shops and cafes with flavorsome coffee and delicious pastries. I'm sure they related with friends, loved ones, and others as well. These thoughts reminded me of how generations are interlinked. As I journaled the following day and later, I wrote about the sameness across generations and their desire to learn from famous architecture, paintings, sculptures, writings, and other forms of expression. A common bond can teach us to treat political, economic, and social differences across cultures with dignity, respect, tolerance, and nonviolence. Thinking about this interconnectedness continues to influence my mindset.

Although we didn't have time to visit Hohensalzburg Castle, we focused our eyes on its location on top of a hill. The medieval fortress overlooks the Old Town and provides a beautiful panoramic view of the greater Salzburg area. Unfortunately, as with other regions of Germany, Salzburg also has remnants of Nazi Germany since allied bombing destroyed parts of the city.

Hohensalzburg Castle from Saint Peter's Abbey and Cemetery

Touring on our own, we revisited Saint Peter's Abbey and Cemetery. The Benedictine monastery, founded in 696 ADS, is one of the oldest in German-speaking countries, and it's still used. Also, the abbey houses the oldest library in Austria. The cemetery, known for its catacombs, has ornate headstones of people buried there.

As I examined the headstones surrounded by decorative fences and manicured gardens, I imagined living in Salzburg in the 1700s. As I read the names on the gravestones and the period these individuals lived, I visualized myself interacting with them centuries before. The same questions I ask myself today came to mind. For instance, what family and personal issues did they face? Which current events did they consider vital? What value did they place on addressing others' welfare and happiness? Would they have acted differently had they had access to social media? Would they have watched soap operas and reality T.V.? Asking myself these questions created a sense of connection, empathy, and appreciation for earlier generations. I think the questions they entertained would be like today's, despite all our technological advances.

Claudia and Lindsey breaking bread

After visiting Saint Peter's, our noses followed the aroma of freshly baked bread toward Stiftbäekerei Saint Peter, Salzburg's oldest bakery. Tucked in a little corner of the Old Town, this oasis of heavenly, tasty delights of freshly baked bread loaves and rolls lured us. I'm sure we would have found it even if blindfolded! Words could not even begin to describe these morsels of yumminess baked daily in traditional fire ovens. Outside the bakery is an original water wheel used to grind flour for the bread. As we snacked on tasty hot rolls, we sat on a bench and watched a video of the bread-making process.

After leaving the bakery, we admired the Baroque steeples as we walked toward the main street of Getreidegasse and the Café

Tomaselli, where Mozart drank coffee centuries before. Founded in 1703, other generations of noted musicians, authors, and artists have frequented the meticulously decorated café. Sitting at a table for four, Claudia and Lindsey imbibed in local tea and pastries as I drank succulent, full-flavored local coffee. Oh yes, we agreed that Salzburg's oldest bakery nurtured our taste buds and very much kept us in the present! It was nice to relax and discuss what we most liked about a city also known for its coffee. Moreover, it was fun watching others resting and cherishing their pastries and drinks. I imagined patrons from earlier periods in history also engaged in similar discussions and enjoyment.

While relaxing, I heard a family sitting nearby speak about Joseph Mohr, a young Austrian priest, who wrote the words to their favorite Christmas carol, "Silent Night," in 1816. Interestingly, the hymn was originally a poem. On Christmas Eve 1818, Mohr brought his lyrics to Franz Xaver Gruber, who composed the melody that same day. Because of flooding in his church and possible damage to the church's organ, Mohr acted urgently to ensure church members listened to Christmas music later that evening. Hence, "Silent Night" was first performed at Saint Nicholas Church, in the Village of Oberndorf, just outside of Salzburg, thanks to Mohr and Gruber's collaboration. I was thankful for learning about my favorite carol while enjoying a thick, creamy cup of coffee. As the family rose to leave, I smiled and said I hadn't meant to eavesdrop, but was thankful for learning about the song's history. They smiled back, saying, "No problem." As Claudia and I had seen years before, patrons greeted one another by saying "Gruss Gott" (Greeting God). As servers bought out the food, they said "Guten Appetit" (Enjoy your meal), and when patrons readied to leave, waitpersons said, "Auf Wiedersehen" (Good-bye). These simple exchanges reminded me of the cheerful times Claudia, and I experienced at our favorite Gasthaus. Upon

Getreidegasse: The main street of Old Town

leaving Mozart's hangout, I thanked our server for reminding me of these memorable moments. Fortunately, she understood my English!

After our brief respite at the Café Tomaselli, we continued our walk in Old Town and stopped at a small shop to buy Mozart's Balls, round chocolate candies of pure delight. Then, as 3:45 approached, we walked toward the tour bus amid the typical traffic sounds of large cities. The cacophony of traffic noise, sirens, and reverberations from construction machinery equated Salzburg with the other cities we visited. However, human verbal interactions, especially laughter, and the sounds of nature, such as birds chirping, helped balance the city's soundscape. Moreover, Salzburg's beautifully manicured gardens, monuments, museums, buildings, and scattering of trees on busy streets added splendor to a city blending its past with the present.

Austrian countryside – I took the picture from our tour bus!

On our journey back to Munich, we again enjoyed and relished the snow-covered rolling alpine countryside. Our tour guide was genuinely knowledgeable of Salzburg and provided us with a detailed history of our visited places. Unfortunately, although Claudia and I had toured Salzburg during my tour in Germany, we didn't remember most of our visit, signifying the importance of journaling regularly.

After bidding farewell to our tour guide, bus driver, and fellow tourists, we walked to the hotel and freshened up. Despite the heavenly delights that filled our tummies in Salzburg, we decided to dine at the Ratskeller in Munich's New City Hall and indulge in an informal atmosphere featuring traditional Bavarian cuisine.

Upon arrival, the place was quite crowded, but fortunately for our hungry stomachs, we were rapidly seated. The establishment has a beautifully designed and authentic Bavarian interior. Proceeding to our table, we passed through dining rooms and halls, hearing laughter and the clinking of knives and forks on plates. Each room had a unique color scheme with tables seating four to eight people. Traditional Bavarian music embellished the atmosphere as mouthwatering dishes soothed and nourished everyone's senses. Claudia and Lindsey ordered tasty schnitzel, and I requested the best sauerbraten I've ever eaten. While dining, we talked about our bus ride through beautiful scenery, Salzburg's quaint streets and architecture, and visiting historic places, for instance, Saint Peter's Abbey and

Cemetery, Mozart's birthplace, and Mirabell Gardens and Palace. Oh yes, Salzburg's oldest bakery topped our list.

Additionally, we interacted with a mother and daughter sitting at a table next to us. The Mom, who lived with her husband in Heidelberg, was visiting her daughter for the Christmas Holiday. The Ratskeller was one of their favorite places to dine. Amid talking to them, we learned the mother was a retired teacher, and her daughter taught English as a second language in Munich. Because I also had taught English as a second language, we shared a common interest, further nourishing our dining pleasure.

What's more, her students' needs, and issues, such as those associated with poverty and immigration, connected her with me. I also found it interesting the daughter followed in her mother's footsteps by becoming a teacher because one of my sisters-in-law pursued her mother's path in nursing. Thus, our commonalities in vital areas of our lives complemented our taste for delicious German fare. After supper, we walked back to the hotel and said farewell to Marienplatz and the Christmas Market. Like the previous night, we surrounded ourselves with other travelers; they, too, relaxed and entertained themselves in the hotel restaurant.

After Claudia and Lindsey went upstairs for a well-deserved slumber, I met an elderly gentleman who had lived in the Philippines with his family. I immediately learned he had been born in Manila during the 1930s and faced the travesty of World War II. As I proudly mentioned my father's deployment to the South Pacific Theatre during the war, his eyes widened. He said he had a deep appreciation for American troops' role in the Philippines, which led to Japan's surrender in 1945. His respect for American soldiers accentuated that, along with Filipinos, they, too, encountered grievous challenges associated with hot temperatures, excessive rainfall, mountainous terrain, and swamps. He explained how these conditions furnished an ideal environment for the spread of malaria. In hearing this, I promptly stated how my father and thousands of other troops contracted malaria via mosquito bites. I could see he, too, had experienced hardships in the war. However, I didn't probe any further because I sensed he would relive sorrowful memories. Sadly, over one million Filipinos are estimated to have been killed in World War II. Also, there was massive physical destruction throughout the islands. Manila, for instance, suffered thousands of human casualties and immense physical devastation.

Who could have known that I would connect with someone sharing the brutality of war with my father at a hotel restaurant in Munich? Besides feeling a close bond with my new acquaintance, I felt a special appreciation and respect for my father, who passed in 1986. For years, I've known he was deployed to Leyte, a Philippine Island, and contracted malaria there. However, I never bothered to ask him about his tour. Had I done this, I could have told him how grateful and proud I was of him for enduring the hardships he experienced.

As I ended my conversation with the gentleman, I expressed how grateful I was for meeting him, shook his hand, and smiled.

> *"If you could only sense how important you are to the lives of those you meet; how important you can be to the people you may never even dream of. There is something of yourself that you leave at every meeting with another person."*
>
> **Fred Rogers**

Because of our 2016 overseas trip, the harmonious trio continues to enrich my perspective and appreciation of people, traditions, and cultures. This has stimulated a mindset that respects differences and tries to avoid prejudging others. Moreover, as I continue with my mindfulness practice, I can more vividly recall past events, such as my observations of the international airports in Paris and Munich and interactions with people and places we visited. Recent research shows mindfulness practice increases short-term memory; my daily experiences over the past few years and my vivid recall of our European vacation, shows that it improves long-term memory as well.

Early the following day, and as Claudia and Lindsey prepared for our departure to Venice, I reflected on our visits to Munich, Salzburg, and nearby areas in my journal. I considered how stillness brings about a sense of tranquility and mindfulness. On our trips to Garmisch-Partenkirchen and Salzburg, the snow-covered landscapes brought about a sense of serenity and deep concentration. I became intensely aware of the beauty I experienced and how it led to joy and happiness. The stillness of the snowy countryside permeated through me and nourished me with a spirit of peace and gratitude. It's essential to balance daily cares and obligations with periods of stillness and respite from everyday activities.

As in other cities, I'm sure Munich's and Salzburg's residents acknowledge the cities' cacophony, such as horns blaring in congested streets, and, without knowing, accept it as a significant part of life. This parallels the subconscious prejudices and biases we all possess and the ensuing emotional turmoil we unknowingly use to separate ourselves from others. Journaling is helping me explore those areas of my life where I may subconsciously detach myself from others for whatever reason.

Before the trip, I usually took pictures to recall places we visited without using travel as an opportunity to journey into my values and beliefs and why I considered them vital. The diversity of cultures, languages, and other areas in the places we visited led to asking myself why I behaved and interacted the way I did. Was I ethnocentric, or egocentric and if so, why? Questioning my beliefs and how I arrived at them was the beginning of a truly transformative journey. Being present and practicing gratitude and compassion toward myself and others enables me to view each day through different lenses. However, my transformation is a life-long journey and requires patience and persistence.

Through personal transformation, I've learned there is often competing traffic in our minds, for example, not being present and sidetracked with unrelated thoughts. This results in not concentrating on the task at hand or enjoying a memorable event, such as visiting Munich and Salzburg. Instead, I've learned that living each day requires active awareness and acceptance of what I perceive or observe. Even in times of challenges, this mindset enables me to view things differently rather than feeling victimized or emotionally distraught.

Undeniably, the Bavarian region of Germany and the alpine countryside of Salzburg are gorgeous. During the 1970s, Claudia and I visited nearby cities, such as medieval Regensburg, Rothenburg, Fussen, and Dinkelsbuhl. Fortunately, they didn't witness World War II's bombing raids and have richness in history and authenticity. Visiting them was like experiencing medieval times.

Although I wasn't profoundly committed to mindfulness practice at the time, I do remember Claudia and I being thankful for an overnight stay in Dinkelsbuhl, noted for its historic moat, towers, and gate. Our hotel was right in the market square and affronted Saint George's Cathedral, built in the 15th century. Our spacious room overlooked both the square and the Cathedral. I remember getting up early the following day and having a breakfast consisting of different types of bread, cheeses, sausages, ham, hot tea, and coffee. Afterward, we held hands and walked around town cheerfully, enjoying its cobblestone streets. Unfortunately, since I had to report back to my unit, we hurriedly left Dinkelsbuhl and didn't have time to immerse ourselves in the town's beauty and history.

Fortunately, Claudia, Lindsey, and I didn't have the same constraints as to when I served in the military, giving us more time to enjoy the scenery and visit where we wanted. Immersing myself in the harmonious trio made my travel even more memorable because I was more deeply aware and appreciative of people and my surroundings. I'm sure I would have learned more about myself and the medieval cities I've mentioned had I more fully engaged in these opportunities as a young adult. For example, during my visit to Dinkelsbuhl, I would have thought of the strenuous labor employed by its builders and gained a deeper appreciation for their demanding work and dedication. I might have also asked myself how I may have responded to the challenges of medieval times. Would there be similarities between their ways of thinking and mine?

Additionally, I reflected on the history of Munich, Garmisch-Partenkirchen, and Salzburg and how people overcame the horrors of World War II. Although dwellers of these cities had political and other differences, something about the human spirit brought them together on the road to recovery and freedom from tyranny. Hopefully, a longing for deep-seated oneness enhanced the reconstruction of buildings and roads. The Essene Tenet I wrote about earlier came to mind: "There is only one of us here. No 'them' and 'us.'"

AUF WIERERSEHEN DEUTSCHLAND!

Chapter 5

City of Bridges

Day 7 (Tuesday)

We embraced our upcoming Venetian visit in the early morning. As Claudia and Lindsey prepared for leaving Munich via rail, I envisioned a safe journey, beautiful countryside, and plenty of camaraderie and laughter between the three of us and others. Many of the trip's moments had already begun to form unforgettable memories. Although visiting iconic museums and monuments was stimulating and thought-provoking, the simple pleasures added value to our trip. Enjoying breakfast with Claudia and Lindsey, eating delicious freshly baked bread in Salzburg, and relishing the beautiful German and Austrian countryside will always be embedded in my memory

Moreover, moments of relating to others from Spain, Germany, and the Philippines enhanced my experience. After filling our bellies with the delicacies of a scrumptious hotel buffet, we walked in a chilly rain that penetrated my winter coat. After a short walk to the rail station, my wet garments joyfully sang, knowing they would soon delight in a warm indoors. Waiting for our boarding time, we enjoyed walking by retail stores, food stands, and mingling with hundreds of individuals traveling to their destinations. As our departure time approached, we went to the platform and waited next to what we thought was the right coach.

Once the train conductor signaled we could begin boarding, we discovered we were on the opposite end of where we needed to be. Hurrying to our coach amid hundreds of other travelers was like Black Friday, with hordes of people rushing into stores to buy reduced sales items for Christmas. To board the crowded train, I gently pushed Claudia and Lindsey up three steps to stand between coaches. The doors closed behind me as I climbed the first step; the train then pulled away from the station. Although happy to have boarded, being squished felt extremely uncomfortable. Unlike Robert Frost's, "The Road Not Taken," I jokingly thought of "The Train Not Taken." We would have avoided the challenges we faced by walking the 566 plus kilometers to Venice or taking a taxi.

In addition to limited breathing space, there was a safety issue. With a sudden stop, passengers might have fallen on each other. Throughout the ordeal, I missed the crying baby from our overseas flight to Paris. At least I sat while crossing the Atlantic. As we left the train station, a couple from the U.S. wanted to join the woman's elderly parents in the next car. As passengers heard their request, they rolled their eyes and remained motionless as anchovies in an airtight sealed container. Some even got annoyed and angry at the couple's request. After several stops and as passengers disembarked the train, the couple finally joined the womans's parents. I must admit I became upset because of being crushed; however, I could have done a better job of experiencing the "here and now" without becoming irritated at the crowded conditions. Instead, I could have paid greater attention to the right things going on around me.

For instance, Claudia, Lindsey, and I sporadically glanced at one another and smiled. I could have also looked forward to finding our first-class seats and appreciated the countryside through windows inviting me to escape my predicament. Heck, I could have conversed with other passengers. A mindset accentuating these possibilities would have lessened feeling irritated, anxious, or stressed. Certainly, unleashing the freedom to participate in the present would have been magnified.

I learned it takes much practice to value the now throughout the trip. Fortunately, each day provides me with opportunities to practice mindfulness and to become more adept at it. It's up to me to make a choice. In Innsbruck, Austria, we found our first-class accommodations; however, others already sat there. We apprised an attendant of our predicament, and he cordially took us to another coach. I figured he wanted to avoid any confrontation with those who took our seats. Ah, yes, it was lovely to sit on previously warmed seats! Soon after, we claimed our first-class seats. As we sat, I realized we would have reached our assigned seats shortly after the conductor signaled to board the train had we waited at the right coach door.

Happily, I didn't wallow in what could have been but looked forward to an enjoyable ride with my wife and daughter. As we relaxed and allowed the Italian countryside to consume us, a young man and woman who lived in Vienna, Austria, joined us in our compartment. We soon discovered they were traveling to visit her mother in Verona, Italy, for the Christmas Holidays. Born in northern Italy, they lived there until accepting employment in Vienna. They liked working in hi-tech industries and living in Austria's "Imperial City." Like us, they liked engaging people of diverse cultures. This helped them understand how others' needs and desires paralleled theirs, thus reducing cultural myopia. It's interesting how this mindset intersected with ours, creating a bond between them and us. Our travel partners enjoyed Vienna's passion for art, music, and international cuisine as well. However, they still loved returning to Italy, visiting its smaller towns, and spending time with their families. Before they deboarded in Verona, we exchanged e-mail addresses. Unfortunately, upon our return to the U.S., we were unable to contact them. Yet, we value the memory of having a meaningful conversation with them.

As we continued to appreciate the beautiful scenery, I read Venice extends across 117 small islands in the Venetian Lagoon, an enclosed bay of the Adriatic Sea in Northeast Italy. It has hundreds of bridges, nearly two hundred canals, and a unique water transportation system with interconnecting bridges. It's called the "City of Water," "City of Masks," "City of Bridges," "The Floating City," and "City of Canals."

Additionally, Venice is famous for its Venetian lace, Murano glass, carnival masks, art, public squares, palaces, and places of worship. Unfortunately, researchers highlight Venice will be underwater within one hundred years because of global warming. Because of future flooding, planning the future is exceptionally urgent. These and other noteworthy facts helped quench the thirst of a history buff.

Our Venetian Welcome

The Venezia Santa Lucia Station greeted us at six o'clock p.m. Feeling calm and well-rested, we walked toward the water bus at the vaporetti station pulling our luggage. We must have looked like unsuspecting tourists when a private guide asked if he could help take our bags to the proper water bus stand. Apparently, we gave him a non-verbal OK,leading to adverse consequences. He took us to a private water taxi costing $100 to reach our hotel destination. After telling him we wanted a less expensive water bus or vaporetti, he hurriedly bought the less expensive tickets at a kiosk. After paying for the tickets, he hurried us to the departure point. In trying to board, we briefly separated from Lindsey as other passengers rushed her into the water bus. As we still stood on the dock, the attendant grudgingly allowed us to board and angrily looked at me. Delaying his departure would have been most unwelcome!

While boarding, I gave him a peace sign, said, "We come in peace," and smiled. As when boarding the train in Munich, it seemed we broke through an impenetrable defensive line for a National Football League team. Yet, Claudia, Lindsey, and I victoriously made it to the end zone and main cabin. As passengers disembarked the water bus, we sat and enjoyed Venice's historic buildings, canals, and lights reflecting on the Venetian Lagoon. I couldn't help but marvel at the city's architecture, built on wooden platforms. Our earlier train ride in Germany was a small price we paid to acknowledge Venice's darkened beauty. When debarking, the attendant even smiled at us.

Certainly, our taxi ride initially seemed messy and challenging. Being in the present includes experiencing inconvenient situations, but not judging them as good or bad. For instance, I could have gotten mad on our train ride because of overcrowding, or angrily yelled at the water taxi attendant. The assumption all moments will be peaceful is an illusion. However, what we learn from them increases wisdom and a greater understanding of how being present can be life-changing. Undeniably, the now influences how we feel, think, say, and do.

Moreover, the water bus ordeal taught me we should have stuck to our original plans. Before deboarding in Venice, we planned to exit the train station, approach the ticket stand, and continue to the vaporetti departure gate. Although we allowed someone to detract from our strategy, we later laughed at our ordeal and acknowledged it as an unusual and unexpected welcome to Venice. Who needed a fifty-piece band and red carpet? Afterall, we benefitted from special, individualized attention plus, we saw the water taxi attendant overcome his anger.

Get Us to the Nunnery

The Best Western Hotel Sant'Elena was about a five-minute walk from the vaporetti gate. The hotel, situated in a quiet, quaint residential neighborhood, is a former convent with nicely appointed, spotless rooms. Our third-floor accommodations consisted of two rooms, a hallway, and a bathroom. The porcelain washbasin was the shiniest I'd ever seen. It seemed someone spent hours polishing it. Lindsey's spacious room overlooked residential homes, apartments, and a narrow canal. It appeared to be a living room area for nuns previously residing there. Claudia and I slept in a separate area spacious enough for a dozen, or so, hobbits. Big, fluffy pillows, and a comfortable bed, soon became our friends. Claudia and I behaved throughout our stay because nuns' "blessed" auras still permeated our room.

After freshening up, we went downstairs in a relatively new elevator. Its cleanliness and efficiency assured us of a fast ride to the modestly decorated lobby. I soon appreciated I could do without many things I thought essential earlier in life. Fancy hotel chandeliers, plush sofas and chairs, elegant curtains, gold-plated dishes, and expensive silverware weren't as vital as spending time with my family and communing with others.

As we ate delicious regional cuisine at the hotel restaurant, we discussed and laughed at the challenges we faced throughout the day. In reminiscing about our train ride, we acknowledged the beautiful countryside, meeting our new Viennese friends, and arriving safely in Venice.

Exploring the Streets of Venice

Next, we walked approximately thirty minutes to Saint Mark's Square. Beginning our stroll, I thought I heard a loud commotion. The loud yells reawakened my childhood memories of the Bronx, where burglaries, muggings, and other violence coexisted with hard working people and young innocent children. I especially remembered instances of people screaming and being physically harmed. As we walked, I didn't say a word to Claudia and Lindsey because I didn't want to alarm them. Moments later, I noticed a soccer game on a large field (Pier Luigi Penza Stadium). What a relief! The shouting came from people rooting for their respective teams.

As I journaled the following day, I accentuated how life's adversities often linger in our minds, although they occurred years before. In my case, shouting from the soccer field reminded me of facing potential daily dangers as a child living in my Bronx neighborhood. Frequently, I feared I'd be mugged or assaulted while going about my daily activities. As I've grown older, I realize it's important to avoid wallowing in whatever misfortune I may come across. It's OK to remember but not imprison myself in anger, fear, resentment, bitterness, or unforgiveness. I can accept life's challenges and respect what I've learned from them, giving me the freedom to consume and learn from the present. In years past, I emphasized what the future may bring as I held on to the past; meanwhile, life passed by me. As I accepted jobs to enrich my future and distance myself from what I thought were others' negative behaviors, I didn't engage the present and enjoy each day as it came.

The street leading to Saint Mark's Square ran along the Grand Canal, Venice's main waterway with beautiful views of centuries-old architecture. The Square seemed like a well-lit oasis in the darkened evening. Along the way, we passed by parks, quaint homes, commercial establishments, and narrow canals. Although we could have taken water taxis, we always walked to our destinations, enabling us to savor canals and structures from the 13th to 18th centuries.

Because of the demanding work of individuals constructing the buildings and canals, Venetians and tourists continue to admire the fruits of their labor. In addition, the different architectural styles, such as Venetian Byzantine, Venetian Gothic, and Venetian Baroque, enhancing the "City of Canals," strengthened our enjoying them. At times, I even touched centuries-old buildings to connect with their builders and history.

St. Mark's Square, Saint Mark's Basilica, the Campanile of St. Mark's Church, and Doges Palace, located on the Banks of the Grand Canal, are in the heart of Venice.

Upon arriving at Saint Mark's Square, or Piazza San Marco, I noticed it hadn't changed much from when Claudia and I visited in the 1970s. Residents, tourists, and pigeons still frequent the area. The pigeons reminded me of my first visit with Claudia. As I photographed the Basilica, a rude pigeon used my head as target practice. That's right! He or she pooped on my head, and I instantly started gagging. After Claudia wiped most of it off my hair, I went into a local

restaurant and used soap to decontaminate myself further. Although Saint Mark's Square is renowned for its magnificent splendor and past, I haven't read about this event in its historical annals. For whatever reason, Venice's officials have yet to ban pigeons from committing these horrific smelly, and messy tragedies! Even today, Claudia and I laugh at the pigeon attack, and if we could find him or her, we'd say thanks for the memory.

View of Saint Mark's Square

Saint Mark's Square served as a convenient access point to places we would later visit: Doges Palace; Venice Theatre, or Teatro la Fenice; and the Music Museum, or Museo della Musica, among other noteworthy places. After visiting the Square, we meandered back to the hotel through pigeon attack-free zones.

Rather than take the elevator to our room, we climbed a simple, tastefully designed marble stairway. Climbing the steps, I thought of how worldwide generations ascended them through the years. The steps, worn from others' footprints, reminded me of how a simple stairway can unite different populations with common aims. Even if a goal is as simple as sleeping in a hotel, we all share areas of interest. By appreciating and respecting these commonalities, we could intensify ways of peaceably relating with others of diverse backgrounds. Desiring and allowing others to separate us wouldn't be as significant. Nuns, the original residents of the convent turned hotel, also used the stairway on their way to bond with their creator and each other via morning, evening, and night prayers. Before this, I thought of using a stairway only to climb or descend physically. Yet, we could also employ it as a metaphor to ascend to a higher, peaceful place, thus overcoming negative biases and prejudices separating us from others.

Sadly, the stairway also could symbolize descending into hatred, bigotry, racism, and sexism. Truly, the hotel's stairway stimulated contemplation. Upon entering our accommodations, our beds and pillows softly whispered, "Come, come, and we'll gently soothe you." Naturally, we obeyed and went to bed early. After all, we had experienced (and survived) our train ride and initial Venetian water taxi ride.

Day 8 (Saturday)

We awoke early Christmas Eve to the serenade of melodious birdsong outside our windows. After getting dressed, our taste buds looked forward to the hotel's flavorsome breakfast buffet of bread, cheese, ham, salmon, scrambled eggs, and other regional foods. The ricotta cheese delighted me to no end! I even made a cheese sandwich by putting it between two slices of parmesan cheese. Savoring such a scrumptious delight caused absolute yumminess! Our itinerary consisted of strolling Venice's streets, visiting the Galleria dell'Accademia, the Music Museum, the Museo della Musica, and Saint Mark's Basilica.

We enjoyed crossing many canals during the day, walking on narrow, winding streets, and the Christmas decorations dotting the city's quaintness. Furthermore, I took pictures to capture the reflection of ancient buildings and bridges, reminding me of Paris' Seine River. Moreover, the gondolas prompted childhood memories and the rowboat rides I took with my father. My father loved boating and how the oars gently made their way through the water's stillness and serenity. Trees sandwiched between the hustle and bustle of congested streets and traffic fumes surrounded our boating adventures. While enjoying the river's tranquility one afternoon, Dad told me how he met my mother as he rowed his boat in a serene lake in Puerto Rico. A sunny afternoon resulted in a romance and marriage lasting almost 50 years until he passed in 1986. At the age of twelve, I saw

One of many appealing canals

their love for each other one summer day. When visiting Howe Caverns in upstate New York, I remember the cool underground and winding limestone corridors with exciting formations and dripping stalactites. As my parents went underneath a kissing rock, I noticed my mother kissing my father, radiating pure love from her eyes. Ah yes, the romance beginning years before continued. The gondolas and boat rides with my father symbolized the interconnectedness of the present with the past. For the rest of our Venetian stay, gondolas reminded me of fond times with my father.

Galleria dell'Accademia

Our first stop, at 10 a.m., was the Galleria dell'Accademia. The museum has an expansive collection of Byzantine and Gothic artworks from the 14th century to the Renaissance era and highlights Bellini, Carpaccio, Giorgione, and Tintoretto. As we passed a security checkpoint, I noticed rules against wearing anything covering a person's head, including helmets. Why a person would wear a helmet in a museum seemed weird. Leaving my baseball helmet back home, I nevertheless wondered if it would have protected me from a pigeon attack in Saint Mark's Square.

As we toured the museum, so did families from other countries. Despite different religions, ethnicities, and races, we valued beautiful paintings and their history. We had similar interests and took photographs of paintings although we weren't supposed to. That's right, some of us showed a rebellious nature, but in a fun way. After about three hours, we walked back toward Saint Mark's Square and ate at a corner restaurant close to the Galleria dell'Accademia and the Music Museum, or Museo della Musica.

After lunch, the soft classical music emanating from the Music Museum welcomed us free of charge. Authentic pianos, violins, and other musical instruments dating back hundreds of years adorned the museum. The beauty and intricacy of each instrument illuminated the painstaking efforts skilled individuals employed in their creation.

Obviously, they took pride in their craft and continue to enrich the ears and lives of music enthusiasts.

Beautiful centuries-old pianos

Background music, which depicted how the various instruments sound, enriched our appreciation of them. At one point, Beethoven's Symphony Number Six, known as the Pastoral Symphony, embellished our visit. Whenever I hear it, I imagine walking in a forest on an early spring day. Along narrow winding paths are budding trees and rivers gently flowing over weather-beaten rocks adorning the forest's magnificent scenery. While on military maneuvers during Germany's iceberg-type winter season, I often escaped by remembering Beethoven's Sixth and imagining such walks. Although I didn't realize it, I possessed the power to make memorable moments in adverse situations. As six o'clock approached, we began our journey back to the hotel.

Heading to our hotel, we visited St. Mark's Basilica. The interior is breathtaking and decorated with bright, gold glass mosaics and marble. The remains of St. Mark, the patron saint of Venice, are contained here. While enjoying our visit, we decided to attend the seven o'clock mass and celebrate Christmas. It was interesting to hear the priest say mass in Italian. I followed what he said because Spanish is my native tongue, and there are similarities between both languages. Although Claudia and Lindsey didn't understand the words of worship, we nevertheless valued participating in a beautiful Christmas event.

St. Mark's Basilica

After mass, we continued our walk to the hotel and enjoyed a clear evening and a 35-degree temperature. Because of our warm clothing, the wintry night air blowing from the Grand Canal didn't freeze us into motionless tourists. Walking by hundreds of strollers loaded with children and baby bags, I wondered if families would go home and

Inside St. Mark's Basilica

watch *A Christmas Story, The Polar Express, Elf, A Charlie Brown Christmas, It's a Wonderful Life,* or other famous movies. Would they open presents on Christmas Eve or Christmas morning? I also remembered my Aunt Asyria making potent eggnog on Christmas Eve. She must have added way more than the recipe prescribed for vodka, making family members and friends thankful for the best eggnog ever!

As the hotel embraced us, Lindsey rested in the room as Claudia, and I relaxed over refreshments at the hotel restaurant. Interestingly, we met a young gentleman from England, visiting Venice with his parents. Like the dynamic trio from Tallahassee, they enjoy traveling together several times during the year. As we talked, he often chuckled, as his shoulders almost reached his ears. His grins and/or smiles reminded me of the Spanish couple I met in Paris.

As he headed toward his room, we exchanged e-mail addresses, and I thanked him for an enjoyable conversation. Interacting with him continued to typify the commonalities many of us have, such as enjoying travel, museums, monuments, different foods, diverse cultures, and meeting new people. It seems if we mindfully search for positive, universal commonalities with others, we can avoid dysfunctional relationships, especially those leading to emotional, verbal, and/or physical violence.

Day 9 (Christmas Sunday)

On Christmas morning, we said a prayer of thanks and exchanged small gifts in celebration. Enjoying our breakfast, we reviewed the day's schedule, including visiting St. Mark's Campanile, the Rialto Bridge, "The Phoenix," or Teatro la Fenice, and the Bookstore of High Water, or Liberia Aqua Alta. Strolling on Venice's streets and enjoying its architecture, canals, and narrow streets always constituted part of our daily itinerary. As I sipped on my cups of cappuccino, I overhead servers talking about how early they left for work that morning. The cooks arrived at five o'clock so they could cook to prepare our delicious breakfast buffet, meaning they boarded the water taxis around 4:30 am, whereas most hotel guests still slept. Several workers celebrated Christmas in the early morning with their families; others would do so later. Although a holiday for some, the work season continued for hotel and restaurant staff, even those with children. As I spoke to a server, she appreciated working on Christmas Day. Despite traveling an hour to work, including riding on a water taxi, she happily supported her family financially. As a young college student and husband, I too worked on many weekends and holidays, but I resented working on these occasions, unlike my server acquaintance. However, I earned money for meeting life's necessities. Immersing myself in conversation with our server reminded me to treasure those moments when I can enrich my family's quality of life.

Upon leaving the hotel, a temperature of 40 degrees Fahrenheit surrounded us. Although the streets were quite empty, several families with Christmas presents walked to visit families and friends, adding to the morning's authenticity. Some families even pulled carts filled with gifts reminding me of my first Christmas in NYC after my parents, sister, and I moved from Puerto Rico. As we walked to Aunt Asyria and Uncle Ruben's apartment, we too carried presents in shopping bags. This was the first Christmas I remember being together with my aunt and uncle and sharing in the merriment of a special day. However, I didn't partake in my Aunt Asyria's loaded eggnog.

St. Mark's Campanile

Our first stop was the Campanile, which is a 323-foot bell tower of Saint Mark's Basilica. The bell tower is free-standing and provides

a stunning panoramic view of Venice. Unfortunately, the Campanile collapsed in July 1902 and was rebuilt soon after. Interestingly, the original Campanile inspired similar towers worldwide, including Slovenia, Croatia, Australia, Germany, and the United States.

As I viewed Venice from atop the Campanile, I wondered about its residents. If I sat at someone's dinner table, what would we discuss? What issues would they bring up? How would they differ from mine?

Bird's-eye view of Venice from Tower

Would some be similar? Would they talk about the latest reality show? By sitting at their kitchen tables and asking these questions, I would have encountered our connectedness and the commonalities we all share. In addition, the beautiful bird's eye of Venice amplified our visit.

Rialto Bridge

As we walked to the historic, centuries-old Rialto Bridge, the sun's rays made for a comfortable holiday as thousands of people filled the streets and many bridges. The stone-covered bridge is a major tourist attraction with shops on either side. While admiring the Grand Canal where it crosses, I imagined how merchants busied their way on this commercial waterway in previous centuries. I even remembered when Claudia and I visited Venice years before and how we enjoyed an evening breeze and long, narrow, jet-black gondolas from the bridge. Now that the harmonious trio engaged my mind, I appreciated the bridge and canal with a deeper, more

Rialto Bridge

intense mindset and realized I was looking at a tourist attraction with greater clarity and focus than in our first visit. Just as the canal and bridge serve individuals by easing travel and commercial activities, we similarly can assist with and care for others' needs and desires, including family, friends, and colleagues. Mindful living helps ensure we do not routinize daily activities and take them for granted. The harmonious trio helps ensure the smooth, and at times difficult, flow of our life's journey.

"The Phoenix," or Teatro la Fenice

The 'Phoenix," or Teatro la Fenice, is a famous, gorgeous opera house. Compositions of Rossini, Bellini, Donizetti, Verdi, Beethoven, Wagner, and Stravinsky have graced audiences in the neoclassical theater. The theater is called The Phoenix because of its exposure to three fires since 1774. As we marveled at the theater's interior, I noticed two of the same families I saw at the Galleria dell'Accademia. However, this time, music brought us together as we smiled and greeted each other. An appreciation for art and music united us, even if just for a moment. This reminded me of a concert Claudia, Lindsey, and I attended in the Summer of 2016. As I looked around the venue, I noticed people of diverse backgrounds and ages applauding and appreciating the singer.

Entrance to Teatro la Fenice

After visiting the theatre, we ate tasty pasta dishes near Saint Mark's Square. The restaurant provided comfortable seating and overlooked part of Doges Palace. A canal and gondolas tied to the sidewalk next to the restaurant reminded me of a familiar photograph. As it turned out, Claudia and I have a picture of the canal and gondolas hanging in our house. The photographer must have taken the image outside the window where we ate lunch. Talk about coincidence! In the middle of Venice, we had a gentle reminder of home. Soft classical music played in the background and enriched the Italian restaurant's ambiance. As our server told us about the day's specials, his face showed indifference. Perhaps his mind was back home with his family, or things weren't going well at the restaurant. Upon sensing this, I pointed to a picture of a cannelloni on the menu, said "yummy," smiled, and said, "I'll have twenty." He then chuckled and, in his Italian accent, said, "Excuse me, my mind is somewhere else," and smiled.

As our server bought our dishes, he delighted in patiently explaining how they'd been prepared and cooked. After eating a fabulous meal, I asked for directions to the Bookstore of High Water. His eyes instantly widened, indicating he really liked the place. As we left the restaurant, I thanked him for our dining experience, shook his hand, and patted him on the shoulder. He smiled back, made eye contact, and said, "molte grazie" (many thanks).

Bookstore of High Water, or Liberia Acqua Alta

The Bookstore of High Water, or Liberia Acqua Alta, nourished us even more. The shop is in a small, quaint, residential neighborhood and has a history of flooding. Thousands of used books in a quirky, narrow, cramped interior beckoned to be touched and read. A gondola loaded with thousands of books inside it highlighted the narrow interior; the books were in no particular order. Many were on either side of the gondola on bookshelves, chairs, and bathtubs. That's right, bathtubs! A sign in the store states, "You don't find the book; the book finds you." Unlike noted corporately owned bookstores,

Where the book finds you!

coffee and snacks were unavailable for sale. Instead, curiosity nourished visitors packed like sardines. As with art and music museums, the bookstore enables people to mingle and examine books of interest. Many seemed captivated by this opportunity.

Strolling on the Streets of Venice

Venice summoned me to photograph canals, bridges, and narrow streets overwhelmed with happy families and festive lights. Plus,

A popular Venetian experience

I took pictures of ornate residences, or palazzos, wealthy Venetians built centuries before to accentuate their wealth. The reflection of buildings, bridges, and lights on the Grand Canal and inland waterways resulted in a double dosage of Venice's beauty and history. Although we didn't buy any Murano glassware, I took pictures by shop windows because Claudia thinks they're stunning. Dedicated master glassmakers have been making their internationally famous creations on the Venetian Island of Murano since the 1400s. As I examined glassware from the first significant European glassmaking center, I thought about how it symbolized generations of expert glassmakers and their passion for creating beautiful artworks.

While approaching the hotel, we walked around the immediate vicinity, consisting of two to three-story apartment dwellings. Some had stores on the bottom floors, reminding me of NYC in the 1800 and 1900s. One apartment had a delightful aroma coming from its open windows; the scent of several spices filled the air and reminded me of my father and mother's cooking. After freshening up in our room, we relaxed in the hotel restaurant and ate a delicious pasta and seafood dinner.

Christmas gifted us with much happiness. I remembered cherished childhood memories, watched families enjoy time together, appreciated how earlier generations developed Venice into the wonder it is today, and saw how music and books brought people together. But, most importantly, I spent precious time with my wife and daughter on a special occasion, the birth of Christ.

Day 10 (Monday)

Each day we anticipated visiting unfamiliar places and learning from them, not of them, as we do via books and other resources. Visiting the Galleria dell'Accademia, Bookstore of High Water, Campanile on St. Mark's Square, and "The Phoenix" supplied opportunities to see how others responded to artworks and artifacts. Furthermore, relating to someone about a painting transcended reading about it in a book, although this too nourishes knowledge. Hand gestures and facial expressions communicated more than words on a page and signaled a desire for peaceful discussion. My enriched perspective altered how I perceived a work of art.

Doges Palace

A visit to Doges Palace highlighted our agenda. We could have spent a whole week admiring the palace's gothic architecture and many chambers adorned with Renaissance Art, such as Veronese and Tintoretto's works. Gilded carvings, murals, and marble floors embellish the palace's interior, including beautifully painted ceilings. Lavish apartments housed the rulers or doges of the Venetian Republic.

Built in the 14th century, Doges Palace was
the seat of the Venetian Republic.

Built in 1602, the Bridge of Sighs, or Ponte dei Sospiri, joined interrogation and courtrooms with a network of small, dark prison cells reminding me of tombs: each contained windowless brick walls enclosing a small, cold, damp, and dark area. Many prisoners sighed upon crossing the bridge, knowing Venice's streets, inland waterways, canals, beautiful architecture, and cultural amenities were just on the other side of gloomy walls.

The musty smell and moisture of the cells elicited several thoughts, such as how prisoners of centuries past must have suffered emotionally, mentally, and physically. Indeed, we should all be held accountable and take responsibility for wrongdoing. However, age-old questions about criminal justice came to mind: Should prisons punish or reform? To what degree should compassion influence the needs of both victims and offenders? Harper Lee's *To Kill a Mockingbird* provides insight. Assigned to defend an alleged rapist, Atticus Finch, the town lawyer, believed individuals should treat others without prejudice. On one occasion, he told his daughter stepping into another's skin enabled you to see things from their perspective and avoid being judgmental.

As I considered these questions, I thought deterrence of criminal behavior and public safety are absolute necessities, but, at what cost to individuals involved? For instance, present-day correction officers perform their duties under stress-inducing situations; many have been attacked and killed by prisoners. These realities make them vigilant about their safety. But stress, anger, and burnout may negatively affect personal and family life. The needs of prisoner safety are crucial as well. Considering these realities, keeping calm in potentially volatile situations is an absolute requirement. I've recently read where there's an emphasis on mindfulness training in correction facilities in parts of the U.S. and Europe. Correction officers learn to be present and attentive to the task at hand, both on and off the job. Some research shows mindfulness enhances job performance and a sense of well-being among officers.

Doges Palace Courtyard

After leaving Doges Palace around 1 o'clock, we spent the rest of the afternoon enjoying Venice and everyone around us. As we headed back to the hotel, we stopped and ate at the Ristorante La Nouva Perla, a local establishment next to the Grand Canal. We ate hot, delicious regional cuisine and chatted with our friendly waiter. I could have eaten several loaves of their mouthwatering bread. Who would have known a combination of flour, yeast, sugar, water, and salt would have resulted in ecstasy? Tons of garlic butter embellished the taste even more. Eating each piece of crusty loaf reminded me of my father baking bread on days off work. He meticulously shaped his heavenly creations into assorted sizes and shapes. If home from school, I'd help him knead the bread until it was soft and smooth. Then I would generously butter the baking pans. As it baked, the bread's aroma spread through our living area and out into the building's hallway, where neighbors partook of its scent. Supper time blended different aromas emanating from other apartments, enticing every-one's sense of smell. After completing our last Venetian supper, we continued our walk to the hotel.

The night lights on the Grand Canal's walkway reflected on the water as glistening stars in the clear, dark sky added to the night's serenity. The scene created a moment I'll long remember. As Claudia and Lindsey prepared for our trip to Florence the next day, I reflected on our Venetian stay.

Because of celebrating the Christmas season, I thought of ways to become a better steward of mindfulness and peace, and the role patience, persistence, and self-compassion play in the process. For example, I remembered getting irritated on our overseas flight. Additionally, I recalled the train ride from Munich to Venice and how passengers grew annoyed (myself included) because of overcrowding and having to stand. However, I thought of the times I didn't get angry, such as boarding the water taxi to the hotel. Unlike the train ride, I adapted and focused on keeping a peaceful and calm attitude. This peacefulness and calmness perpetuated itself by immersing myself in the present. I genuinely enjoyed listening to and learning about the Viennese couple's enjoyment of art and music and how they relish visiting Italy during the holiday season. I remembered looking outside at the beautiful, calm, peaceful, moving countryside as we conversed as well.

Communicating with hotel staff, restaurant servers, museum staff, and others added to the value of connecting with people and embracing life's moments. These individuals' commitment to their families and a hard work ethic demonstrated how these attributes joined people from diverse backgrounds, regardless of differing values and beliefs. Randomly meeting people constituted one of the best parts of our Venetian stay. Partnach Gorge's snowy, ice-covered scenery came to mind as well. The hills on either side of the Gorge resembled tips of icebergs; they represented only a fraction of what we admired. What lay below their surface was unseen by human eyes. So often, we're unsure what motivates others because their values and beliefs lie within them. Frequently, I've allowed hidden negative prejudices and biases toward others to confine me. Without knowing, I've imprisoned myself inside the dark, cold, damp prison cells of Doges Palace. Fortunately, the harmonious trio's daily practice and this travel memoir have helped free me from my unfortunate, regrettable prison sentence.

Moreover, I learned a lot about gondolas and gondoliers from a gondolier himself. Waiting for Claudia and Lindsey one afternoon, I spoke to a gondolier wearing the traditional attire of a striped shirt (either black or red stripes), black pants, shoes, and a straw hat. He praised his work, even if it included long hours at certain times of the year. Additionally, he enjoyed breathing the water's salty air and valued that every canal has a different sound based on its narrowness, width, and proximity to buildings. I asked him if it was difficult to steer a gondola since he only used one oar to maneuver it from the back. He remarked the difficulty varied according to the narrowness of canals, the height of bridges, tight turns, and traffic volume. In inclement weather, he needed to carefully maneuver on choppy waters, which at times was challenging. In addition to being skillful in these areas, the gondolier was required to speak English and know routes to Venice's landmarks. Although he wasn't a good singer, he sang to alert other gondoliers when turning corners. I could tell he was proud of following his family's tradition. Because of transportation advancements, tourists now primarily use gondolas. I learned many aspects of his profession by reaching out and attentively listening to him, thereby, enriching my Venetian experience. If I hadn't spoken to this gentleman, I'm uncertain whether I would have researched gondolas' vital role in Venice's history. Clearly, we have the power to embrace and create unforgettable moments! It's a choice we can make daily.

Incidentally, after our return to the U.S., I learned the gondolier profession embodies current worldwide challenges associated with gender and women's issues. It wasn't until 2010, a 24-year-old female, who wanted to follow in her father's footsteps, became the first woman gondolier in a centuries-old industry governed by men. In 2017, the first transgender male of German and Algerian descent won a court battle to operate a gondola for a hotel chain. These two incidents remind me of being patient and persistent in pursuing our goals. These two attributes are essential components of the harmonious trio.

In addition, I tried to cheer the places we visited regardless of their lavishness or simplicity. Our hotel room's shiny washbasin, fluffy pillows, and comfortable bed gratified me. I had never seen such a shiny porcelain washbasin! Yet, our view of nearby apartments and a canal interested me most. I wondered about the canal's history and the stories behind the multitudes of people who used it to travel.

Similarly, I reflected on the lives of people living nearby. I'm sure the issues they meet are like those of others around the world. Finally, looking at the apartment windows, I reflected on how an appreciation for simplicity can bring about happiness.

Although I enjoyed the gilded carvings, murals, and marble floors of the Doges Palace, I considered our home's simplicity. No amount of gold and silver could ever replace the peace and happiness we enjoy in our simple abode. The memory of raising our daughter here far exceeds any lavish dwelling. I'll never forget Lindsey coloring and writing on a simple wooden pine desk as she wished me a "Happy Fathers' Day" at eight years old. Unquestionably, being aware and appreciative of my family and surroundings is resulting in fond memories and gratitude for being present.

Being present also includes how I relate to people and settings at any moment. One day at our Venetian hotel, I said hello to an elderly house cleaner vacuuming a room. Her half-moon dark eyes and face exuded accumulated wisdom stemming from the different seasons of her life: ones of happiness, sadness, kindness, anger, forgiveness, unforgiveness, grief, unconditional love, and others. I also noticed extraordinary perseverance and kindness gleaming from her eyes. Upon reaching the stairway, I heard her sing as she went about her chores. It seemed regardless of past experiences, good and bad, she controlled the present and treated others with kindness through her work and other areas of her life. This and other Venetian encounters deepened my commitment to mindful thinking. Indeed, it requires the daily application of patience and persistence to ensure it continues to grow as a driving force.

ADDIO VENEZIA!

Chapter 6

Birthplace of the Renaissance

Day 11 (Tuesday)

A sunny, breezy morning greeted our imminent departure from Venice. St. Mark's Square, narrow canals, winding streets, and other iconic features bid farewell while enjoying our thirty-minute water taxi ride to the central train station. Because we stood outside the cabin, we relished the whistling wind blowing softly against our faces as the boat gently cut through and pushed canal waters to the side. The sprinkling of white, wispy clouds over us reminded me of Partnach Gorge and our tour to Salzburg. When the taxi made its scheduled stops, workers hurriedly boarded on their way to work. Just as the cab made its way through the water, passengers made their way through life. Passing St. Mark's Square, I couldn't help but smile about my pigeon encounter years before and how I laughingly shared this memory with Lindsey. I also reminisced about our Venetian stay and memories that would long endure.

Although we could have rented a car to sightsee and for photo ops, it seemed traveling by train would be less nerve-wracking. I'd also read train travel was inexpensive and a convenient way to travel around Italy. Because of high-speed trains, day trips from Rome to Milan and Venice are possible. Boarding our train at approximately 10 a.m., we knew exactly where to go and sit. What pleasure this proved to be! We were becoming seasoned travelers in Europe! Like our train ride the week before, we saw beautiful hillsides, homes, and steeples as we rode in a southwesterly direction from Venice. The ride only took approximately two hours.

Like in air travel, we put our lives in the hands of total strangers and assumed we would arrive safely to our destination. While immersing myself in the countryside, I thought of procedures to ensure proper maintenance of locomotives, rail cars, tracks, and overall travel safety. Also, I thought of the people involved in these processes and the risks and hazards associated with their jobs. Furthermore, safeguards must address the safety of rail tracks, train crossings, railroad switching, proper speed limits for various weather conditions, and population densities.

Thinking about these details, I remembered a taxi ride we took several years earlier from LaGuardia Airport in Queens, New York, to our hotel in downtown Manhattan. Speeding on East River Drive, the driver talked on his phone rather loudly and zipped in and out of traffic lanes. Claudia and Lindsey closed their eyes to escape from his reckless driving. On one occasion, I suggested he may want to slow down because we worried about his driving speed, but to no avail. As he talked on his phone, it seemed he was practicing for the

Daytona 500. I did write a letter to his taxi company in 2003, a few weeks after the incident occurred. Unfortunately, since they have yet to respond, I doubt they will anytime soon.

Although vital modes of transportation are heavily regulated, there's always room for human error, in addition to mechanical and technical malfunctions. However, I trust pilots, train conductors, and other personnel are well trained and rested before departure, even though risk factors that may imperil safe travel are present. Otherwise, how else would I travel overseas, in the US, and other parts of the world, including my community? In the case of overseas travel, would I paddle a boat or take a cruise ship? So, it seems I must somehow reconcile my comfort level, knowing there'll always be risk factors associated with safe travel. However, the same applies when crossing a street, walking in a parking lot, sitting at a movie theater, and doing other activities. In each of these instances, the element of trust is of profound importance. I should confide in the ability of others to help ensure my safety, even if just crossing a street.

Building trust in all areas of our lives is a difficult challenge. Unfortunately, many of us (myself included) don't always trust we can peacefully commune with others, even strangers. Because of this mindset, we may fail to learn of others' cultures and attributes because of our biases or prejudices. Many of us negatively respond to stereotypes we consider harmful. Consequently, we deprive ourselves of developing meaningful relationships to further our mental, physical, emotional, and spiritual well-being. Our train ride from Venice to Florence stimulated these thoughts. Just like well-trained locomotive personnel help promote safe travel, the harmonious trio can help ensure we meaningfully live each day with appreciation and a willingness to learn about ourselves and others non-judgmentally.

The Santa Maria Novella Train Station is in the heart of Florence. It's one of the busiest in Italy and a short distance from some of its major attractions. The various levels of the station include banks, a restaurant, and a drug store. Outside the station, travelers have access to bus lines that carry them across Florence and other cities and towns in the Tuscany region.

Florence is the capital city of the Tuscany region. It has approximately 400,000 inhabitants and over 1,520,000 people living in the metropolitan area. Moreover, it's the birthplace of the Italian Renaissance (14th through 16th centuries).

Walking to the hotel, we marveled at Florence's charm and authenticity. After all, it was the cradle of the Renaissance, noted for its history, magnificent monuments, churches, museums, narrow streets, and its association with famous writers, painters, sculptors, and inventors. Although German troops occupied Florence from 1943 to 1944, the New Zealand Army and South African Troops liberated it in 1944. However, the city didn't suffer from the travesty of massive bombing raids.

The Residence La Contessina is family-owned and in central Florence. It's a beautifully restored hotel with an outside patio surrounded by a variety of plants and flowers. The reception clerk, who was very personable and friendly, quickly checked us in. Upon our request, she reserved tickets to the Academia dell'Galleria and the Uffizi Gallery the next day, saving us considerable time and effort.

Opening the door to our room, we became amazed at its spaciousness and layout. Soft colored walls and a loft with a single and double bed accentuated the room. The downstairs living room area showcased terracotta floors, with a small kitchen to the side. Artwork on the walls depicted various Florentine scenes and impressively enhanced the room's attractiveness and serenity. A sofa, dining table, coffee table, and a couple of end tables invited us to sit, relax, and nap with outstretched feet. These were the most pleasant, coziest, and comfortable accommodations of our trip and ensured a wonderful way to end our journey. I even got to exercise because the bathroom was on the ground level. You know, those late-night bathroom visits enabled me to go up and down the stairs and burn some calories! Oh yes, the room could have accommodated dozens of hobbits with plenty of dancing space. They even could have slid down the banister rails for fun!

Patio inside hotel

After unpacking and freshening up, we ventured outdoors into Florence's historic center at two o'clock. Being hungry, we decided to eat at the Da Nerone restaurant, approximately one hundred feet from our hotel. When entering, we became enthralled by the restaurant's ambiance, sculptures, and paintings. The menus, one in Italian and one in English, highlighted Tuscan food and, oh yes, pizza and calzones! For an appetizer, we ordered Bruschetta and immediately devoured it once placed on our table. For our main courses, Claudia and I shared a cheese pizza, and Lindsey ate a calzone. Talking about living on the wild side! What can I say? We love pizza and calzones, especially me! The food and service were outstanding, and complimented the restaurant's authenticity. The server readily understood my Spanish and a little of my English. As in Venice, I often spoke in Spanish because of its similarities with the Italian language. Before leaving, we decided to return later in the week for supper. After lunch, we enjoyed walking on quaint streets and visited the Piazza del Duomo and Dante Alighieri's House Museum, or Casa di Dante.

A view of the restaurant

Duomo

One thing about Florence, most of its historical places are within easy walking distance of the city's center. The Piazza del Duomo is no exception. The Santa Maria del Fiore Cathedral, Baptistry of Saint John the Baptist, the Campanile, and Museo dell'Opera del Duomo are in this highly ornate complex. After walking only ten minutes on narrow streets, dotted with Christmas decorations and many passersby, we arrived at the Cathedral, named after St. Mary of the Flower. The name signifies the lily, the symbol of Florence. Construction began in 1296 and took over one hundred years to complete.

The Santa Maria del Fiore Cathedral's Gothic architecture and its colors are unequivocally unique. Its distinctive geometric pattern with white, green, and pink shades of Tuscan marble and orange dome accentuates the exterior. While admiring such a magnificent structure, I marveled at what the human spirit could accomplish. Like the architect of St. Michael's in Munich, the Cathedral's designer lacked formal training in architecture. Consequently, modern mystery surrounds how Filippo Brunelleschi, a goldsmith and clockmaker, drew plans to build the world's largest masonry dome. After his death, no one found his blueprints for the Cathedral. Of particular interest is how he engineered the eight-sided dome so it wouldn't collapse during construction. This is of vital interest because there wasn't any central support system.

Santa Maria del Fiore Cathedral

Moreover, researchers have yet to determine the technology employed in constructing the dome, including lifting four million bricks, weighing approximating 37,000 pounds. In addition to being Florence's hub, the Cathedral symbolizes Brunelleschi's imagination and creative genius; no wonder he's one of the Renaissance's seminal figures. The Santa Maria del Fiore Cathedral's iconic dome exemplifies and magnifies the human spirit's vitality. At the Piazza, we bought tickets to the historic buildings later in the week.

Strolling on the streets of Florence and Dante Alighieri's House Museum, or Casa di Dante

After our sneak preview of the Piazza del Duomo, we continued sightseeing amid hundreds of fellow pedestrians cramming the narrow streets. Interestingly, the center of Florence is a World Heritage Site with church bells and traffic noise filtering through the streets. Storefronts and outdoor vendors greeted passersby with on-the-go street eats, including tripe (stomach of a cow) with tomato sauce, Porchetta (boneless pork roast), Panini (small bread rolls with meat and cheese), Lampredotto (stomach of Bovine), and gelato. Throughout our stay, mouthwatering gelato and its variety of flavors helped highlight our day. Similar to Venice, Munich, Salzburg, and Paris, tired pedestrians filled the streets as late afternoon approached. Despite this, store clerks invited shoppers to peruse expensive, colorful winter clothing and shoes. After all, Florence is one of the world's fashion capitals.

Dante Alighieri's House Museum, or Casa di Dante, was conveniently located and easy to find. The three-floor house museum, holding his life's works, is on a quiet, narrow side street in the heart of medieval Florence. Nearby was the church he attended. Dante, a poet, scholar, painter, and philosopher, used his worldview to canvas his imagination. As a high school and college student, I remembered studying how Dante's *Divine Comedy* is an allegory of human life depicting the Christian afterlife. Its three narrative poems-Inferno,

Purgatorio, and Paradiso-warn society to avoid corruption and steer toward righteous living. Dante's sense of the afterlife touched on compassion, lust, gluttony, greed, fraud, betrayal, and violence, which still permeate society.

Observing Dante's house museum visitors, I thought of the written word being a bridge uniting generations, including young and old. Centuries later, Dante's *Divine Comedy* brings people together in appreciation and respect for his writings. However, his house and museum reminded me we could use writing to justify our negative prejudices and biases. As a humanities and social studies teacher, I urged students to use the writing process to determine whether their content explicitly, or implicitly, justified racism, hatred, sexism, or violence. This strategy also would increase critical thinking skills, which are severely missing today. One of my major aims was to increase awareness of our commonality with others and grow as a peaceful society by treating individuals with dignity and respect regardless of background. Although many students received A's in other courses, many hadn't used writing to learn about themselves.

Because of *The Gift of Travel*, I've been learning about various methods to exude compassion toward others; some strategies are scientifically driven. However, our trip to Dante's house and museum reminded me of a spiritual approach to compassion. His quote, "Compassion is not a feeling, but rather readiness of soul to perceive love, mercy, and other virtuous feelings," challenges us to show compassion toward others. The study and practice of compassion are multifaceted and very much needed in society. Not going to Dante's house and the museum would have been a lost opportunity; it wouldn't have triggered a deeper appreciation for his writings. Upon returning to the U.S., I re-read the *Divine Comedy* and developed a more profound commitment to practicing compassion and an intense realization of how greed, fraud, betrayal, and violence hinder building peaceful and healthy relationships with others.

Because seven o'clock was approaching, we decided to dine at our hotel's café, La Sosta delle Contesse. However, we revisited the Santa Maria del Fiore Cathedral to appreciate its splendor further. The night's fog blended beautifully onto its white, green, and pink shades of color. However, our tummies soon beckoned us to continue walking, and so we did.

Entering the café, its atmosphere and simplicity impressed us. A server led us to a room overlooking the dark, narrow side street and neatly parked bicycles and motor scooters. An elegantly designed long wooden door, weighing several hundred pounds, embellished the building across the street. Pictures of food from the Tuscany region adorned the light-colored walls as dark wooden beams crossing the ceiling added to the simple yet elegant atmosphere. Once seated, we studied the menu, highlighting Tuscan specialties and a local favorite, Florentine T-Bone steak. After exploring our options for a few moments, we ordered a delicious appetizer, savory supper, and drinks. Because of the servers' charm and the restaurant's quaintness, we decided to return there for our last Florentine supper on Friday.

Day 12 (Wednesday)

Although we dined only twelve hours before, we anxiously looked forward to breaking our fast. Our first hot tasty breakfast of scrambled eggs, ham, cheese, and croissants was delicious and fueled our bodies for the day's activities. My three cups of cappuccino were the best cups of caffeinated, milky, frothy, and steamy happiness I ever tasted. Breakfast enabled us to reflect on the previous day's activities and plan for the current day, including touring the Academia dell'Galleria, Uffizi Gallery, and Piazza della Signoria. Laughing and being together always highlighted any given moment.

Academia dell'Galleria

The Academia dell'Galleria, our first stop, is home to Michelangelo's statue of the Biblical David and his four sculptures of "Slaves" or "Prisoners." There are also exhilarating collections of paintings from the Middle Ages, Renaissance, and the early part of the 17th century. We grew in anticipation entering the brick building with rounded windows. Shiny marble floors and arched hallways, decorated with sculptures and richly colored paintings adorning brightly painted walls, embraced us. Our primary goal was to see the statue of David.

Nearing the statue, I remembered writing academic papers about David and other masterpieces in the Academia dell'Galleria. Recalling these undertakings, suddenly, there he stood in all his magnificence! What can I say? Even if I exercised 24/7, there's no way I would have David's body tone. The statue, Michelangelo's depiction of David just before his Biblical battle with the giant Goliath, was created between 1501 and 1504 from a large marble block. The slingshot David holds is relatively small. To me, it signifies being victorious over Goliath, not because of physical stature or weaponry, but of being in the present, self-confident, and determined.

Statue of David

Interestingly, Michelangelo believed a sculptor's purpose was to create and reveal what already existed inside a marble block. For instance, David's entrance hallway has four of Michelangelo's unfinished statues, collectively known as "Prisoners" or "Slaves." Scholars have named them the "Awakening Slave," "Young Slave," "Bearded Slave," and "Atlas Slave." According to some art historians,

Atlas Slave

each statue symbolizes individuals trying to free themselves from material trappings and other challenges. The fact they're unfinished symbolizes it's a life-long effort.

Concentrating on the statues, I thought about the trappings and other challenges I've faced. Many are like those included in Dante's *Divine Comedy*, including violence and lack of compassion. Identical to other individuals, violence in the form of verbal, emotional, and physical abuse has often confronted and challenged me. When my family and I first moved to the Bronx, we were among a few Puerto Rican families living there. I soon learned non-Hispanics didn't necessarily welcome us.

Consequently, others called me derogatory names like "spic," which worsened to low self-esteem and poor academic performance because English wasn't my native language. Furthermore, since we didn't have formal instruction in English for Speakers of Other Languages (ESOL), I learned to read English independently, which negatively affected my academic performance. Subsequently, teachers labeled me a lazy and slow learner. In addition, my sixth-grade teacher told me I wouldn't amount to anything after performing poorly on English and Math tests. Because of these challenges, I grew in anger, bitterness, and resentment toward myself and others.

After graduating high school and like Michelangelo's "Slaves" or "Prisoners," I began chiseling out of the marble I allowed others to hold me captive. As I grew older and matured, I remember reading books and articles on self-worth, positive thinking, anger management, inner and interpersonal conflict resolution, and spirituality. Claudia's unconditional and enduring love has also played a crucial role in freeing me from my self-imposed prison term because of how others treated me. She's taught me forgiveness, kindness, and compassion toward myself, and others, are essential ingredients for living a fruitful and joyous life. Like the prisoner statues, I continue to free myself from the harm others imposed on me. However, I'm also releasing and forgiving myself for the hurt I've caused others. As with David's statue, it's not physical stature that eases this liberation; freedom comes from increased awareness of the present, self-confidence, and determination. Moreover, like David, my belief in God and his teachings enables me to travel peacefully through life's journey and achieve fruitful outcomes.

Reflecting on Michelangelo's four statues, I was thankful for how they reminded me of the challenges I faced as a youth and the trials millions of people continue to undergo because of religious beliefs, ethnicity, and other demographic traits. Interestingly, a by-product of reflecting on Michelangelo's works was how the harmonious trio made our stopover more exciting and impactful. In reflecting on the statue of David and the "Four Prisoners", or "Slaves", I was also grateful for the opportunity to see them firsthand. Otherwise, my ability to reflect and learn from them may have been limited. Moreover, empathizing with the challenges millions of people confront because of cultural and religious differences quickened my compassion toward them.

Michelangelo also sculpted the "Rebellious Slave" and the "Dying Slave." The Louvre in Paris houses them. Although we could have spent an entire week or more appreciating the Academia dell'Galleria, our stomachs decided it was lunchtime. Consequently, we left the gallery that nourished my appreciation for the world's most prominent painters, sculptors, and thinkers.

"Prisoners" leading to David

Our scheduled time to the Uffizi Gallery was 2 p.m., which gave us ample time to partake in a relaxing lunch. After crossing the Arno River, we discovered a quaint basement restaurant named il Cantinone Osteria on Via Santo Spirito. Upon entering, we soon encountered charming arches and beautiful brickwork. The ambiance and friendly, prompt service complemented our dining pleasure. The appetizer, consisting of mussels in a white wine sauce and garlic, was incredibly delicious; dipping our bread into the sauce intensified our satisfaction even more. Next, Claudia ordered scrumptious lasagna, oozing with melted cheese, and Lindsey requested mouthwatering pasta with chicken and sweet tomato sauce. As they lovingly consumed their dishes, I indulged in a healthy bowl of soup teeming with beans, sausage, potatoes, and other vegetables whose seasoning made my taste buds dance in pure glee. Finally, the two foodies devoured a decadent, creamy layered dessert with chocolate syrup. While dining, accordion music highlighted by traditional tunes, including Quando, Amore, and Volare, played in the background enriching the restaurant's ambiance. I imagined a musician playing his accordion at our table and devoting each push and pull to the three of us.

Folks enjoying time together at the il Cantinone Osteria

Uffizi Gallery

After lunch, we went to the Uffizi Gallery, another world-famous art museum containing indescribable art masterpieces: Michelangelo's "Doni Tondo;" Giotto's "The Ognissanti Madonna; Botticelli's "La Primavera" and "The Birth of Venus;" Raphael's "Madonna of the Goldfinch;" Titian's "Venus of Urbino;" Uccello's "The Battle of San Romano;" Caravaggio's "Bacchus;" and Lippi's "Madonna with Child and Two Angels."

Other paintings and sculptures adorn a long labyrinth of rooms seeming to run for miles and miles. In addition to works of art, the interior walls and orna- mented ceilings made my

One of Uffizi's beautiful corridors

eyes pop out of my head. The building housing the Uffizi was con- structed in the 1500s and originally housed Florence's administrative and judiciary offices and is next to the Piazza della Signoria.

Uffizi has beautifully painted ceilings

In our outing to the Uffizi and Accademia dell'Galleria, I intensely appreciated artists' ability to create an image initially visible only in their mind's eye. Several artists of the Renaissance era were scholars and skillful in several art forms. For example, besides being a renowned sculptor, Michelangelo possessed in-depth knowledge of the human body, which is evident in his masterpieces, for instance, the Sistine Chapel, the statue of David, and the Pieta. Indeed, he and other famous individuals of the time, such as Leonardo Da Vinci, encapsulated one of the Renaissance's central tenets: the "thinking man."

Da Vinci wrote about anatomy, astronomy, geography, physiology, medicine, sculpture, machines, and warfare. Having a multi-faceted mindset enabled him and others to view the outside world using comprehensive lenses, which enriched their understanding of humanity's interconnectedness. Granted, we need experts in our lives. For example, if I needed brain surgery, I'd want a well-trained surgeon conducting it, not an auto mechanic or English teacher. But, although I understand few individuals can master several specialties in medicine, engineering, law, information technology, and other fields, compartmentalized thinking may limit seeing the big picture.

During my career, I usually looked at the big picture. As a human services policy analyst, I conducted needs assessments and strategic planning in education, housing, law enforcement, employment, health and medical services, and other human services. Although each sphere required a certain degree of compartmentalization, effective strategies in one field needed to overlap with others to ensure a comprehensive approach. An effective long-term big picture strategy to increase educational attainment for middle schoolers, for instance, included access to affordable health care, a suitable living environment, nutritional food, efficient transportation, viable employment for parent(s), and other areas of vital concern. A big picture approach also required collaboration with experts in each field to arrive at cost-effective solutions.

In some cases, if one or both parents were incarcerated or unavailable, strategies also addressed the added responsibilities of grandparents because they often helped raise their grandchildren. In addition, a big picture approach aided a child with achieving successful test scores and learning essential skills. Research clearly shows how disadvantages, such as suffering from nutritional deficiencies, not getting sound sleep because of inadequate heat, and hearing domestic altercations between parents, affect academic performance. Because of my exposure to the human services arena, I applaud the talents of Michelangelo, Da Vinci, and other famous Renaissance artists, painters, sculptors, and thinkers. Their mindsets facilitated their ability and desire to understand and portray the world using the multifaceted lenses of their disciplines. An appreciation and respect for the interconnectedness of the world and its inhabitants illustrate the importance of enriching one's perspective of people worldwide. Our tours of the Accademia dell'Galleria and the Uffizi strengthened this outlook.

Although I realize the importance of specialists addressing my needs, I find it helpful to learn about other disciplines, thus enriching my worldwide view. Because of our trip, I've taken art classes and learned about different musical styles. I'm also increasing my knowledge of philosophy, sociology, science, psychology, and medicine. Although I'm grateful for these opportunities, I'm also thankful you'll never have me as your brain or heart surgeon!

Piazza della Signoria

After leaving the Uffizi Gallery, we entered the nearby Piazza, an open air gallery, having a replica of David and other statues of historic Italian figures. In addition to being mesmerized by the gallery, we watched others as they too valued what the historic setting offered.

Piazza della Signoria

Additionally, a young female singer with a beautiful operatic voice and an accompanying organist cast a spell on those present (me especially!). Her spellbinding voice enchanted us for approximately an hour. What a treat she was to the crowd she so skillfully and lovingly entertained! Her intonation, hand movements, and facial expressions connected with the public as she synchronized with the organist. I especially appreciated her Italian rendition of "Granada," a song about the city of Granada in Spain, written by the Mexican composer Augustin Lara in 1932. Besides enjoying it sung in the open-air gallery, I especially relish it if it's played on a flamenco guitar.

The singing of Lara's "Granada" also reminded me of Michelangelo's "Prisoners" or "Slaves." I thought of how composers' and artists' creations may reveal what has already developed in their minds and need expression via music, paintings, and sculptures. And here a young millennial connected with music written in the 1930s in a historic Renaissance setting. Once again, the present joined with the past and vice versa.

Day 13 (Thursday)

In Paris, we arranged for a bus tour of Tuscany. The day finally arrived. Once the hotel owners learned about our bus tour, they suggested we eat before our morning departure, even if it meant breakfasting before official restaurant hours. Upon hearing the owners' suggestion, I immediately thought it was out of genuine concern and respect for our needs. Their caring attitude seemed like a heartfelt consideration for others' well-being, not because we were paying guests at the hotel. We responded to their kindness by knocking at the restaurant's front door at 6:45 and delighted in a hot delicious breakfast. Afterward, we walked to the tour buses in front of the Santa Maria Novella Train Station. About seventy tourists boarded two tour buses at approximately eight o'clock for the day-long adventure, including sightseeing in the Tuscan countryside, Siena, San Gimignano, and Pisa.

Tuscany

We soon began appreciating Tuscany's gently rolling hills, still dipped in a soft morning mist soon dissipating from the sun's warmth. Located in north-central Italy, the Tuscany region is breathtaking. Riding toward Sienna, our first destination, we loved the beautiful landscape dotted with golden wheat fields, olive groves, vineyards, medieval hilltop villages, castles, small towns, and rolling mountain ranges in the distance. In addition, Tuscany has bed and breakfasts or B and B's, farmhouses, hotels, villas, and apartments available to accommodate tourists. Traditional central Tuscan cuisine includes tomatoes, meats and fish, pecorino cheese, pasta, and delectable sauces.

Siena

We soon approached Siena after reveling in the stunning Chianti Hills of Tuscany. The bus driver parked outside the town, and as we began walking toward the historic medieval center, I was hypnotized by beautiful medieval architecture. Interestingly, Siena has been subdivided into ten wards since medieval times. An animal or mascot represents each. Rivalries among the wards are most evident during the *Palio* annual horse races held in the Piazza del Campo. Yes, the Piazza is that big! The Mangia Tower overlooks the Piazza and appreciative onlookers. Unfortunately, we didn't have ample time to climb its stairs and celebrate the surrounding view.

Siena, in Italy's Tuscany region, is the capital of the province of Siena. Declared by UNESCO as a world Heritage Site, it's famous for its art, museums, and medieval cityscape.

From the Piazza, our tour guide accompanied us to the Siena Cathedral, or Duomo. The intricate design of Italian Romanesque-Gothic architecture was candy to my eyes! According to our tour guide, the interior has an inlaid marble mosaic floor, which is the most elaborate in Italy. In addition, famous Sienese masters, like Donatello, Lorenzo Ghiberti, and Jacopo della Quercia, adorn the Cathedral with their artworks.

Piazza del Campo, built in the 13ᵗʰ century, is in Siena's center

After viewing the Cathedral, we walked on quaint narrow streets and passed by the Gothic-style Basilica of San Domenico. This magnificent brick structure and bell tower sit in a prominent location of Sienna. Moreover, the remains of St. Catherine of Siena, one of Italy's two patron saints, are found here (St. Francis of Assisi is the other patron saint). Because of time constraints, we took pictures of the centuries-old Basilica and went back to our tour bus.

Siena Cathedral or Duomo

Interior of Cathedral

San Gimignano, or *The Town of Fine Towers*

After leaving Siena, we rode to San Gimignano, a small medieval, walled town resting on a hilltop in the province of Siena. In addition to its medieval history, it's famous for its wineries. We stopped at one and partook in a lunch of pasta and salad, in addition to tasting several varieties of wine. We sat at long picnic tables between wine vats and graciously partook of all the delicacies and liquid cheer. I also spoke to a family from New Delhi, India. In between eating bites of our food, I told the father how much I admired India's architecture, for instance, the India Gate, a historical landmark in New Delhi, and the Taj Mahal outside the city in Agra. I also mentioned some of my favorite Indian food, especially potatoes and peas in curry. The father and I were especially thankful for Italy's cuisine and the country-side. It turned out we had a common interest in urban development because of our city and regional planning backgrounds. Once again, Claudia, Lindsey, and I related to a family with shared interests and an appreciation for Italy's food, architecture, and countryside. Our conversation significantly added to a delicious meal!

After lunch and wine tasting, the group boarded the tour buses for a short five-minute ride to *The Town of Fine Towers*. From a distance, San Gimignano's towers looked like a medieval skyline. Stopping at the UNESCO World Heritage Site overlooking Tuscany's rolling hills epitomized stepping back in time. All we needed were suits of knightly, shiny armor, swords, and plate armored horses to enhance the atmosphere.

The medieval city of San Gimignano

Entering the walled town, I imagined myself as Sir Michael the Great and Knight of the Round Table. However, my new status was short-lived after tripping on a cobblestone, thus ending my escape into fantasyland. Instead, I resumed my tourist role amid Romanesque and Gothic architecture. Somehow, my sweatpants and jacket didn't conform to the status of a prominent, seasoned knight.

There are about 1,500 inhabitants in the walled medieval town of San Gimignano; approximately 7,500 live in the surrounding area. The town, known for its pottery and ceramics, overlooks breathtaking Tuscan scenery and renowned vineyards.

Although its narrow cobblestone streets added to San Gimignano's authenticity, modernity was also present. Restaurants, cafes, and shops sell clothing, souvenirs, delicious gelato, and other flavorsome treats. Claudia, Lindsey, and I bought gelato at a small, crowded shop and walked to an outlook overlooking the Tuscan countryside. While eating our delicious treat, we delighted in the beautiful scenery. However, our schedule soon overtook our stay, and we returned to the tour bus.

Pisa

Our next and last stop was Pisa, approximately five miles from the Mediterranean Sea. The Arno River, which flows across Florence, also runs through Pisa. After getting off the tour bus, we walked to the Piazza dei Miracoli, or Plaza of Miracles, a UNESCO World Heritage Site. This walled-in medieval plaza contains the Leaning Tower of Pisa, which leans approximately four degrees. In addition, the Pisa Cathedral, the Battistero, and the Camposanto Monumentale, also located here, are exceptional examples of medieval architecture.

Pisa is a city in the Tuscany region and is known for its leaning tower. In addition, it has more than twenty other historic churches and medieval palaces. About 92,000 people live in the city.

For a panoramic view of the city, visitors to the Leaning Tower may climb 297 steps to its top. Unfortunately, time constraints and a long waiting line prevented us from ascending. Besides, my legs felt like spaghetti noodles because of all the walking we had done during the day. We did, however, get to see each of the other historical places in the time allotted. That's one thing about taking tours: a tight schedule. However, we cheered others tilting their hands, pretending they were holding up the Leaning Tower, as another person snapped their picture.

Leaning Tower of Pisa

Despite our brief stay, we thoroughly appreciated our stopover. I especially valued the architecture and the illuminated medieval buildings at sunset. Like the tour leader in Salzburg, our guide's knowledge and people skills were exceptional. A native of Florence, he had led tours for approximately five years. Most of his training was by learning firsthand from knowledgeable and skilled guides. His enthusiasm and respect for his job were quite evident. Before leaving Florence, he at once made us feel comfortable. In addition to conveying facts about the places we stopped at, he told stories about them, making the tour more appealing. It was interesting to listen and learn from a Tuscany region resident instead of learning about it in secondhand accounts. For each place we visited, he also recommended his favorite establishments to eat and drink. Oh yes, he was very patient; he didn't mind if tourists asked him questions after already covering the answers. What's more, his love for Florence's writers, such as Dante Alighieri, Francesco Petrarch, and Niccolò Machiavelli connected with me. We instantly connected when we agreed Dante's *Divine Comedy* is one of the most remarkable pieces of literature in history. Interestingly, he worked at Dante's house museum in his late teens.

After arriving in Florence, we walked back to the Residence La Contessina, freshened up, and returned to the Da Nerone restaurant. Why reinvent the wheel? Afterall, hot regional meals teeming with heavenly, delectable, mouthwatering, and luscious morsels of food awaited us. We shared the Bruschetta while Lindsey indulged in a plate of delicious ravioli. As Claudia rejoiced in her pasta with alfredo sauce, I consumed tasty, hot steamy mussels with red wine sauce. Once again, we were charmed by the restaurant's ambiance, friendly service, gorgeous interior, and simple, yet succulent cuisine. Afterward, we walked to the Piazza del Duomo and entered a nearby locally owned bookstore. As I meandered around the store and surrounding area, Claudia and Lindsey examined what seemed hundreds of books as my tired feet, and I patiently waited.

Day 14 (Friday)

On Friday morning, we ate an early breakfast (it seemed we had just eaten, but that's how it is for the two foodies in my life) and walked to the Santa Maria del Fiore Cathedral, our first stop of the day. In addition, our itinerary included the Campanile di Giotto, Baptistry of Saint John the Baptist, an archeological dig, and Museo dell'Opera del Duomo. Later in the day, we would take pleasure in the Rose Garden, or Giardino delle Rose, Piazza Michelangelo, and the Piazza della Repubblica. We also would enjoy Florence's narrow streets, Christmas ornaments, shops, architecture, and people. Beginning each day with a cheerful outlook, we looked forward to enjoying and learning from the places we would spend time at. We connected with others via simple smiles and waves; after all, they constituted part of our experience. As each day progressed, our attitude overcame our tired feet while readying for a relaxing evening.

Santa Maria del Fiore Cathedral

The Cathedral has an austere interior typical of the Florentine style of the time. Forty-four stained glass windows stood out, as did the works of Michelangelo and Donatello. Mosaic floors enrich the grandeur of the world's fourth most prominent Roman Catholic Church. Additionally, the Cathedral features "The Last Judgement," a fresco originally painted by Vasari. Long aisles reminded me of Notre Dame Cathedral and Saint Patrick's Cathedral in New York City. As I looked at others, I noticed they, too, were fascinated by the Cathedral's architectural splendor.

Inside Santa Maria del Fiore Cathedral

Campanile di Giotto

The time came to hike up the Campanile di Giotto, a free-standing bell tower next to the Santa Maria del Fiore Cathedral. The "Stair Way to Heaven," as I like to call it, is a long, narrow, spiraling stairway consisting of 463 steps. However, there are several landings where people can rest and appreciate the Campanile's interior, parts of the Piazza del Duomo, and a panoramic view of Florence. When climbing the stairs, individuals can get a closer view of Giorgio Vasari's frescoes of the "Last Judgement." Oh yes, there's no elevator.

After reaching halfway to the Campanile's top, Claudia suggested Lindsey and I climb the remaining stairs, and she would sit and wait for us. Not being in good physical shape, I soon grew weary, tired, sweaty, and thirsty. As hundreds of other tourists climbed each step along a narrow spiraling staircase, some stepped to one side holding their breaths, so others could descend back to planet Earth.

Finally, we arrived! After 463 steps and my loss of twenty pounds, Lindsey, and I savored a breathtaking, panoramic view of Florence, its terracotta rooftops, and surrounding hills. I thought of how the surrounding countryside must have looked centuries before the city's population sprawled outward. Our way down wasn't too challenging, which was OK for us. We soon met up with a well-rested Claudia, the pilgrim who decided against a magical climb to the heavens. Incidentally, we had already bought tickets to climb the four hundred plus steps to the Santa Maria del Fiore Cathedral's dome. After asking

Claudia and Lindsey if they were still up to it, they smiled and said, "No thanks, we're good!" Upon hearing this, my legs and I felt an extraordinary bond with them!

Panorama of Florence from Campanile

Climbing the Campanile once again reminded me of how important it is to respect and appreciate earlier generations' efforts. As Lindsey and I enjoyed the panoramic view from the tower, I recalled a picture of workers eating and sitting on a steel beam of an unfinished Empire State Building in the early 1930s. One individual seemed to be focusing on New York City's panorama hundreds of feet above the ground (not me, thank you!). As he looked, I imagined him having the opportunity to link with past, present, and future generations. Perhaps, he thought of and was grateful for the thousands of workers who helped build surrounding buildings, streets, parks, museums, and theaters. Without knowing it, he left an imprint connecting with me 80+ years later. One of my first jobs was in the Empire State Building. Like many other individuals, I went to work and put in my time. Unfortunately, I didn't think highly of the role construction workers played in build-

Looking at the outside world from our gelato paradise!

ing this iconic structure. I failed to consider how past generations enriched my quality of life and didn't consider leaving a meaningful imprint for future ones.

After visiting the Cathedral and climbing the bell tower, we treated ourselves to gelato at a nearby café. The mouthwatering silky richness of the Italian-style ice cream soothed our tired feet and thirst. Once I found out gelato has less fat than ice cream, I almost ordered another bowl. Interestingly, its taste seemed more intense than ice cream. As we consumed our creamy bowl of happiness, we amused ourselves, watching the passersby for about thirty minutes of rest.

Baptistry of Saint John the Baptist

After gelato time, we spent time at the octagonally shaped Baptistry of Saint John the Baptist, or the 'il Battistero di San Giovanni. Saint John is Florence's patron saint. Situated in front of the Santa Maria del Fiore Cathedral, the Baptistry exemplifies Romanesque architecture with green and white marble. A pyramid-shaped dome with eight triangular sides adorns the top of the Baptistry. Before entering the east side of the Baptistry, I photographed a replica of Lorenzo Ghiberti's famous gilded bronze door, "The Gates of Paradise," sculpted between 1425 to 1452. The door has several panels depicting critical Biblical events, such as the story of Jacob and Esau. Likewise, Ghiberti's other bronze sculptures are awe-inspiring, especially for art history enthusiasts.

The Baptistry's interior has beautiful works of noted Florentine artists. A

Gates of Paradise

mosaic of saints and Biblical scenes with Jesus covers the ceiling. Interestingly, Dante and other notable Renaissance figures, including members of the Medici family, were baptized here. As we sat, the three of us reflected on the Baptistry and its history. While doing so, I thought of how baptism symbolizes renewal and cleansing. The sprinkling of, or immersion in water, highlights the event. Considering this, I thought of how our trip symbolized a baptism, resulting in personal renewal. I tried to look at each day using the lens and sprinkling of the harmonious trio. Similarly, I recalled Michelangelo's "Prisoners" and how they exemplified cleansing myself from life's trials and tribulations.

Archeological dig

Next, we explored an archeological dig beneath the Cathedral of Santa Maria del Fiore. The dig, lasting from 1965 to 1973, has

Michelangelo's Florence Pieta

what remains of Santa Reparata. Construction workers rebuilt this ancient Christian Basilica several times before erecting the Cathedral of Santa Maria del Fiore. Walking through the remains supplied an opportunity to understand the significance and implications of Florence's history fully. Relics of the city's past came to life as gravestones of noted religious leaders and other noted individuals, such as Filippo Brunelleschi, added to the dig's historical significance. Beautifully designed mosaic flooring and original fragments of walls caught people's eyes. As I admired the dig, I thought of how it's vital to preserve the past. For example, Brunelleschi's tomb wasn't discovered until 1972, even though he died centuries before. Fortunately, preserving history and learning from it are embedded in the minds of archeologists, historians, and other specialists. In addition, physical evidence of human ingenuity, for instance, the Piazza del Duomo, in conjunction with documents I examined in museums, magnified my appreciation of Florence's history.

Museo dell'Opera del Duomo

After exploring the Santa Reparata archeological dig, we went to the Museo dell'Opera del Duomo. The museum, which added to a pleasurable day, featured Michelangelo's "Florence Pieta" and Donatello's "Mary Magdalene."

Both creations suggest the significance of seeing with the mind's eye and its vital role in both artists' lives. Studying these sculptures, I realized artists must have the gift of imagining specific images or scenes and conveying them into masterpieces. After all, the sculptors and painters whose works we esteemed in Paris, Venice, and Florence didn't have any templates to follow when creating their iconic works. Instead, like maestros, they orchestrated their skills and imagination to transform marble and blank canvasses into beautiful and memorable artworks. Therefore, after several centuries, we continue to respect and connect with their genius and creative masterpieces. Indeed, famous artworks and memorable moments in my life are valued gifts linking past and present. I have an immeasurable appreciation for both.

After seeing the Museo dell'Opera del Duomo, we consumed a mid-afternoon lunch at a nearby quaint restaurant at approximately two o'clock. There was a row of tables along each side of the extended, narrow seating area. Each table, covered with white linen tablecloths and Chianti bottles, gave the establishment an authentic Italian feel. Pictures of Florence

Donatello's Mary Magdalene

adorned the walls as we enjoyed a pleasing view of the Piazza del Duomo. The melted cheese from our pizza oozed from each slice as our tongues danced in merriment. Unlike other Florentine restaurants, our ears danced to the merriment of American Rock and Roll.

We began walking toward the Arno River on the Via dei Calzaiuoli, a central street in Florence's historical center, linking the Piazza del

Duomo to the Piazza della Signoria. Christmas adornments and festive, multi-colored twinkling lights on streetlamps, shops, restaurants, and cafes enriched a jubilant atmosphere and Christmas spirit. Although we already visited famous places on this street, we never grew weary of them. The statues and architecture in the Piazza della Signoria continued to entertain hundreds of persons. Numerous holiday concerts awaited locals and tourists throughout our stay.

Several bridges cross the Arno River: Ponte alle Grazie, Ponte Vecchio (no cars allowed), Ponte a Santa Trinita, Ponte Carraia, and Ponte Amerigo Vespucci. The Ponte Vecchio was the only bridge not destroyed by the German Army during World War II. Similar to the Seine, it's value-added walking along the scenic Arno. Arriving at the River, Claudia, Lindsey, and I crossed to the Oltrarno area, a historic and authentic site consisting of narrow winding streets dotted with small stores, cafes, and restaurants. Oltrarno translates to on the other side of the Arno. We explored the area earlier in the week to eat at the quaint, small basement restaurant I previously mentioned. Many storefronts displayed wood carvings, sculptures, and paintings as artisans showed their skills to passersby. Ceramic hand-painted plates, vases, kitchen utensils, and oil bottles depicted the Chianti region and its beautiful landscapes.

Arno River

Rose Garden, or Giardino delle Rose

The Rose Garden, or Giardino delle Rose, was first on our list of places to see in the Oltrarno area. A narrow, winding, and steep road led to it. The scenery and rustic buildings on both sides of the road were stunning. Trees enhanced the landscape on our walk to the gardens. Unfortunately, we couldn't explore them; although they closed at 5 o'clock, ticket sales stopped at 4:30. To think we could have discovered the gardens' beauty by depriving ourselves of cheesy, mouthwatering triangles of deliciousness! Oh well, we still indulged ourselves in a panoramic view of Florence and its surrounding countryside from the site.

Heading back down the winding road, we passed by a young lady walking uphill toward the gardens. I apprised her they closed at

The street leading to Giardino delle Rose

5 o'clock, and she at once thanked me for saving her from a wasted trip. The four of us then walked downhill and learned a little about each other. She and Lindsey hit it off quite well. We said our goodbyes at the bottom of the hill since she visited our next destination earlier in the day. She was a very charming person from Milan and was sightseeing in Florence for the Christmas holiday. Had we toured the gardens, our paths may not have crossed. If so, we wouldn't have spent time with each other, even for a short period.

Piazza Michelangelo

The Piazza Michelangelo, built in 1869, was a major destination. Our ascent involved climbing steep stone steps with beautiful trees on either side of the broad stairway. Upon reaching the top, we reveled in a spectacular view of Florence while orange rays of sunset filtered from the sky. The early night air enhanced the ambiance as gorgeous lights lit up Florence and its surrounding countryside in breathtaking fashion. Hundreds of locals, tourists, and vendors filled the Piazza, and yes, a bronze statue of David graced the area. That guy gets around in Florence! It was interesting to watch workers construct a stage for New Year's Eve the next night. Several musical groups would entertain thousands of revelers then.

View of Florence from Piazza

After an hour or so, we decided to meander back to the hotel for our last Florentine supper. Along the way, we crossed Florence's most famous bridge, the historic Ponte Vecchio, built in the 13th century. The stone arch bridge, filled with merchants selling jewelry, artworks, and souvenirs, is like Venice's Rialto Bridge.

After crossing the Arno River, we passed by the Piazza della Repubblica, yet another time. The Piazza is a city square and known for being Florence's first forum. Political discussions, debates, and meetings took place here; furthermore, it served as a marketplace. Locals, including noted artists and scholars, still meet at the Piazza's cafes.

Piazza della Repubblica

After arriving at our hotel at about eight o'clock, we freshened up and went to the hotel restaurant, where we requested an appetizer of delicious mussels from Southern Italy. For our main course, we ordered our long-awaited Florentine T-bone steaks, or Bistecca alla Fiorentina. The meat from the Chianina cattle, raised in Tuscany and nearby regions for almost 2200 years, is famous for its quality and nutritional value. Claudia and Lindsey ordered grilled vegetables with their steak, and I ordered roasted potatoes with mine. As our server delivered the steaks to our table, he said, "buon appetito," (enjoy your meal) and we certainly did! Claudia and Lindsey shared their T-bone steak as I consumed one by myself. Smiling in sheer, mouthwatering delight, we cut into our steaks as our widened eyes absorbed such edible beauty. The juicy, lean, tender, medium-rare, steaks melted in our mouths. Thousands of my tongue's taste buds fought each other to get the most from each succulent bite. Who knows? Maybe I was developing into a foodie myself! Claudia and I also savored a scintillating fruity white wine from Sicily. Other customers laughed and, related to each other, thereby enriching the restaurant's warm, cozy atmosphere. After dinner, we returned to our hotel room, got a good night's sleep, and prepared for leaving the next day.

Day 15 (Saturday)

Our last morning in Florence was bittersweet. Although we looked forward to returning home, a part of us (at least me) wanted to prolong our trip. Perhaps a year or so? After breakfast, we bid farewell to our excellent hosts, boarded a taxi to the Florence Airport, or Aeroporto di Firenze-Peretola, formerly named *Amerigo Vespucci*. Our driver talked on her cell phone during our fifteen-minute ride as we passed by older and newer parts of Florence. Unfortunately, certain aspects of modern technology prevent us from meaningfully conversing and relating to others.

At the international airport, we checked our luggage, passed security, found our gate, bought souvenirs, and snacked at a cafeteria with a distant view of Florence. Colossal glass walls throughout the airport blended the interior with the outside, creating a feeling of openness and highlighting it's a gateway to Tuscany. Bright lights reflected off silver columns and brightened seating areas. An adjacent rail station with trains going to Pisa and other parts of Italy and Europe reminded me of the one in Paris. Looking at the destination sign to Pisa, I smiled, remembering our stop earlier in the week. Finally, the time to board our jet with connecting flights to Orlando arrived.

Our stay in Florence presented a memorable way to end our trip. Along with the many masterpieces we took pleasure in, the historic medieval city illustrated how the arduous work of creative geniuses, including Michelangelo, Leonardo da Vinci, and others, produce intergenerational linkages through art, music, literature, and architecture. As in Paris, we walked the very streets these famous figures did years before and felt connected with them, even centuries later. Additionally, these individuals' creative geniuses must have involved deep concentration while engaging in their creations. They undeniably manifested attributes of mindfulness and its patient and persistent application. For example, some historical documents mention da Vinci took long breaks when painting *The Last Supper* to allow his imagination to express itself. His intensity of commitment has intrigued millions of admirers across the centuries.

Just as Florence is the cradle of the Renaissance, I thought of how individuals could be the cradle of their personal Renaissance. In her book, *On Becoming an Artist*, Ellen J. Langer, a noted Harvard psychologist, writes, "Creativity and mindfulness are natural partners. Understanding how to think mindfully is the best way to break through the roadblocks that keep us from developing our creative selves."

Indeed, conscious thinking increases my creative juices; for instance, I never thought of authoring a book before the trip. However, by pausing at various museums, including Dante Alighieri's House Museum, I began removing roadblocks I allowed some teachers to place before me. I remember how a college writing instructor questioned my ability to write creatively and suggested I seek other ways to express myself after the fifth week of class. I took what he said to heart and never bothered to become a writer. However, I never thought of how his evaluative criteria limited my ability to succeed. Instead, I allowed him to restrict my freedom to choose a writing career. In going to Dante Alighieri's House Museum, I realized I mindlessly listened to the teacher's advice and didn't seriously consider becoming a writer or pursuing other avenues to expand my creativity. My immersion in Dante's works and other creative masterpieces of writers and artists enriched my commitment to write this memoir, and along with an intensified allegiance to the harmonious trio, I've become absorbed in a personal Renaissance.

In Florence, I better understood that mindfully engaging in gratitude and compassion requires focused determination. Besides appreciating time with Claudia and Lindsey and all the city offered, I became increasingly grateful for activities I often took for granted, such as walking, eating, breathing, washing my hands, and enjoying others around me. Although I was sometimes distracted with hunger, thirst, tired feet, and other things, I learned to return to a state of mindful behavior and increased gratitude. The Academia dell'Galleria and the Uffizi Gallery supplied opportunities to express sincere appreciation for opportunities to see beautiful masterpieces. Michelangelo's "Four Prisoners" at the Academia dell'Galleria remain entrenched in my mind. Whenever I find myself stressed or frustrated, I fondly remember what I learned from them: they symbolize how we can meaningfully address life's travesties.

Although I didn't count the number of times I smiled at others, it seemed my "smiling frequency" significantly increased since leaving Venice. As others smiled back, I reflected on how small mindful acts proved we could relate to others with kindness and compassion. Gandhi wrote, "You must be the change you wish to see in the world, even if it's just one step, or smile, at a time."

In Florence, I devoted more time to meditating in the morning. A brief 15-minute meditation session, helped prepare me for the day, resulting in greater awareness and appreciation of the present. Still, it wasn't easy; while meditating, my mind often wandered, and instead of being calm and relaxed, I impatiently judged myself for not focusing. Daily meditation remains challenging because random thoughts often distract me. Thus, developing a healthy and fruitful meditation practice requires much patience and persistence.

Furthermore, our Florentine holiday enabled me to compare it with the various cities and countries we explored. I realized how things I hadn't taken pictures of stood out the most. The hot, creamy crepes we relished eating in front of the Eiffel Tower in below-freezing temperatures remained a highlight of that day. Claudia and Lindsey's deep slumber blessed each day's end and brought immeasurable joy. The breakfast salmon and several types of cheese embellishing our stay in Munich brought back smiles and a hunger for more. Our conversation with the young couple traveling to Venice, eagerly awaiting their future together, reminded me of my early married years.

Additionally, I pondered how the museums in Venice bought individuals of diverse backgrounds together and how an appreciation for art and music helped unite strangers in a spirit of peace and harmony. Shaking hands with total strangers linked generations of distinct cultures and exemplified how we can live as one despite differing backgrounds. Finally, church bells ringing throughout the day in medieval Florence quickened my appreciation for what we experienced. They reminded me of how fortunate we were for embarking on our trip.

Listening to the melodic sounds of church bells ringing, I thought of how the harmonious trio is like a maestro synchronizing the present movements of my cognitive, emotional, physical, and spiritual well-being into a well-orchestrated symphony. As a maestro, the trio blends the past with the present and the present with the future. It shows how the trials and tribulations of intergenerational life experiences can help bring people together. It's up to strangers and non-strangers alike to choose between oneness with or separation from others.

"The future is being made out of the present, so the best way to take care of the future is to take care of the present moment."
Thich Nhat Hanh

ARRIVEDERCI FIRENZE!

Chapter 7

Our Return Home
and
What Now?

After boarding in Florence and making ourselves comfortable, we watched others maneuver down narrow aisles. Several passengers desperately tried to stuff their carry-ons into the overhead bins. Some almost re-packed their suitcases! Fortunately, flight attendants facilitated the process, and we climbed the friendly, welcoming sky in a timely fashion.

During the flight, the complicated infrastructure of airports and the complexity of airplanes consumed me. Each year, billions of suitcases and other items go through airports. An elaborate setup helps ensure people's possessions promptly make it to the right place. However, one technological mishap on a conveyor belt can have a ripple effect on hundreds, if not thousands, of travelers and their cherished luggage.

Ensuring efficient passenger flow at check-in counters, security checkpoints, and throughout an airport is of utmost concern. I thought of how "Travelators," or moving sidewalks, are available at many airports to prevent passengers from bumping into each other as they scramble to their departing gates. Moreover, I've traveled on what I call the "plane train" at Atlanta's Hartsfield International Airport. Well-trained personnel control the movement of these underground trains to guarantee prompt access to the airport's terminals. Similar transportation systems exist at major airports worldwide.

As if an airport's infrastructure isn't complex enough, imagine the complicated structure of large airplanes, such as an Airbus A380. Thousands upon thousands of rivets and hundreds of miles of wires support essential communication and proper movements of the plane's fuselage, wings, and rudder. Furthermore, the knowledge and skill level needed from pilots, flight attendants, technicians, medical staff, air traffic controllers, and emergency specialists are vital considerations. Additionally, I reflected on what it takes to prepare meals for overseas travel and the hundreds, if not thousands, of workers involved in the process.

Moreover, I noticed a certain calmness on the plane. Although I would have been grateful for these precious gifts, there weren't any crying babies. However, it was nice to have moments of tranquility while confined to tight quarters and narrow aisles. Unlike the flight to Europe, I had a more positive, grateful, and calm attitude. In addition, I thought of all the blessed moments with Claudia and Lindsey and was thankful they sat next to me.

Day 16 (Sunday, New Year's Day)

Nearing midnight, we landed at Orlando International Airport, got our luggage, and checked into the airport hotel. Two comfortable, friendly, and welcoming beds greeted us and wished us "Happy New Year" as we entered the room. We quickly succumbed to their warm embrace.

The New Year presented me with a greater appreciation for the effect mindfulness, gratitude, and compassion would continue to have in my life. The places we visited, the scenery we relished, and the people we met were like the North Star leading me to a more fulfilled and joyous life. It's gratifying to visit places physically, relate to people face-to-face, and experience their mannerisms first-hand. These actions further active engagement and increased awareness and appreciation of ourselves and others.

It's empowering to be unafraid of expressing our thoughts by peacefully saying what we think of small things. We can then build up to profoundly meaningful conversations without emotionally, verbally, or physically abusing others. For instance, the Socratic method encourages us to ask and answer questions without judging what others think, thus increasing our critical thinking ability and helping us to avoid negatively interacting with others. Unfortunately, the Socratic method and critical thinking usually are not emphasized in schools and other environments. A sensitive, diplomatic mindset, including peaceful, effective communication skills, is needed in our communities because we're united through a unique universal oneness despite cultural and other differences. In those cases where financial and other constraints may inhibit travel, journeying through books, museums, documentaries, magazines, virtual travel, and other sources can nourish our quality of life.

When you recover or discover something that nourishes your soul and brings joy, care enough about yourself to make room for it in your life.

Jean Bolen

Mindful Living

Jon Kabat-Zinn's *"Wherever You Go, There You Are"* highlights being present in whatever we're doing and not wising we were executing something else. Throughout our journey, I overheard families complain about their trip and past vacations. In some cases, parents were planning for upcoming holidays and stressing over them. Meanwhile, their children were busy playing by themselves, not being engaged by Mom or Dad. Sadly, past and future concerns undermined enjoying the now, robbing families of more cherished memories.

In "Beautiful Boy (Darling Boy)," John Lennon sings, "Life is what happens to you while you're busy making other plans." During Lindsey's childhood, there were many times I could have been with my family but instead chose to work. In addition, I was consumed by "what ifs." "What if I'd taken another job?" "Why didn't I get a promotion?" "How come I'm not getting a salary increase, but she or he is?" As these thoughts lived rent-free in my mind, present moments went right past me. Because some of my job positions were grant-funded, I often thought, "What if funding stopped?" "Would we have enough savings for Lindsey's college education, assuming she'd want to attend?" "What if we needed to place our parents in an assisted living facility or nursing home?" "Would we have enough to facilitate paying for it?" These concerns remind me of Mark Twain, who wrote, "I have been through some terrible things in my life, some of which actually happened." Hearing about others' anxieties and complaints in hotel lobbies and restaurants made me sincerely appreciate togetherness with Claudia and Lindsey and enjoying new experiences. Furthermore, the positive vibes of others counterbalanced hearing resentments, frustrations, displeasures, and other negativities.

> *Life is now. There was never a time when your*
> *life was not now, nor will there ever be.*
>
> **Eckhart Tolle**

Preoccupation with things that may never happen interfere with the practice of mindfulness. Minor distractions hinder appreciating everyday life as well. Traffic congestions, being interrupted in conversations, not being thanked for comforting someone, misplacing my favorite baseball cap, others' rudeness, getting a flat tire, and other occurrences perturbed me immensely. Mindfulness practice plays a vital role in alleviating these harmful, toxic reactions. If someone cuts me off on the highway, I try to empathize with the driver and make allowances for their behavior. Perhaps the individual is going through a stressful situation and not fully aware of what they're doing. Regardless of their state of mind, their behavior shouldn't interfere with my mental and emotional well-being.

If I'm getting irritated, frustrated, or angry, I gently remind myself of my imperfections and that learning to live in the now is not a quick, painless process. It requires the patient and persistent practice of forgiving myself and self-compassion. Our train ride from Munich to Venice and passengers (myself included) annoyed because of overcrowding and standing comes to mind. My so-called discomfort made me insensitive to the couple from the U.S. and their desire to join the wife's elderly parents in the next coach. Waiting 15 minutes for service at the hotel restaurant in Munich resulted in unjustly judging the server as unreceptive to my selfish desires. Reflecting on these events, I acknowledged my quick-to-judge attitude and lack of patience.

I thought of mindfulness's critical role in forgiving myself and self-compassion throughout the trip. As I continue to forgive myself for my imperfections, mindful behavior empowers me to see life through holistic, contemplative lenses instead of an uncompromising perspective emanating from my ego. In past years, my self-centeredness prevented me from understanding and respecting others' viewpoints. As a result, I didn't fully engage and relate with others, which closed doors to personal, professional, and spiritual enrichment. However, the gift of mindfulness continues to open doors, thus overcoming these shortcomings and stimulating lasting change.

Being present has rippling effects in all areas of my life, even if least expected. Visiting St. Mark's Basilica and appreciating its gorgeous interior led to unplanned participation in the seven o'clock Christmas Mass and resulted in a blissful, fruitful experience. The marble stairway at our hotel in Venice was analogous to the ups and downs we experience throughout life. By climbing up or going down each worn step, I thought of the stairway's authenticity and the countless footsteps comprising its history. Each step supports the aspirations and shortcomings of people worldwide and unites past, present, and future generations. My unplanned conversation with the gondolier led to a rewarding discussion, including gaining better regard for his profession and skill set. This wouldn't have happened if I had not focused on our dialogue. Plus, our conversation led to fond memories of my father and his love of boating.

As doors to increased mindfulness widen, I appreciate the importance of how past and present generations impact lives. Because of engaging others and exposure to superior works of artists, musical composers, writers, philosophers, and religious teachers, I understand, more than ever, we all have commonalities despite our many differences. The creative genius of individuals, such as Da Vinci, and his heightened commitment to conscious living, continue to link generations. His fascination with interdisciplinary study, and his observation of people and the environment, help ensure people with different talents and interests connect with his works and each other regardless of age.

Fortunately, calmly associating with others is foremost in many people's minds. However, individuals and groups hate and disparage others because of certain characteristics, thus uniting them in a common cause. Unfortunately, these behaviors are gaining substantial momentum. Yet, studies show how to overcome behaviors leading to injustice, discrimination, and violence. Surely, we can mindfully employ these strategies on a personal and group level and become more peaceful, caring, and loving. There are numerous resources we can use toward this end.

Like the famous individuals I've written about, we, too, can leave a legacy of mindfulness through daily practice and modeling. Like brushing our teeth and dressing every morning, we can groom our morning mindset to emphasize peacefully interacting with our family, others, and the environment. Communicating with the mother and daughter in Munich, the young Italian couple, a young man from England, the gondolier, and my father's counterpart from the Philippines, inspired me to continue stepping out of my old comfort zone and understand others through their eyes and not my subjectivities. The French author, Anaïs Nin, writes, "We do not see things as they are; we see things as we are."

Every moment supplies the freedom and opportunity to practice mindfulness; our visit to Florence offers a clear example. One afternoon, when waiting to cross a street, the red light allowed me to become fully aware of my surroundings and experience the now. Rather than looking for the time, I seized the moment by noticing people, sounds, and smells, enabling me to mindfully step out of automatic pilot, even if just briefly. Small moments like these lead to an enriched mindfulness practice.

Meditation became a close companion of mindfulness throughout our trip and furthered gratitude and compassion. Meditating daily significantly enhances my inner peace by preventing or alleviating emotional turmoil, such as anger, stress, frustration, and resentment. Although there're many meditating styles, they all lead to improved mental, emotional, and physical well-being. Its practice enables me to connect with myself and enhance staying present on any given day.

Moreover, mindfulness and meditation ease breaking from harmful patterns of thinking and behaviors. Being liberated enhances bonding with others and my quality of life. Research shows mindful living and meditation cause a rewiring of our brains, thereby improving overall mental, emotional, and physical well-being. In my case, I'm sure my rewiring encompasses thousands, upon thousands, of miles (and then some!).

Although I have a long way to go, I've become increasingly conscious of my journey toward more profound mindfulness. For instance, I reflect on attitudes and behaviors enriching or interfering with my transformation through journaling. I ask myself how I'm treating loved ones, neighbors, friends, and acquaintances. Am I showing respect and concern for them? Am I critical of others, and if so, why? How am I dealing with criticism? The list goes on. Thankfully, I'm tracking my progress by manifesting the harmonious trio and joyfully remembering the seeds I've been nourishing since our trip.

Gratitude

While writing this travel memoir, I sincerely appreciated the gift of traveling overseas with my family. I was extremely grateful for being together and thankful to the pilots, flight attendants, museum personnel, artists, sculptors, architects, train conductors, hotel reception clerks, cooks, tourist guides, etc. But, unlike Christmases past, these presents didn't come in a box.

As I compared my culture's nuances with those of France, Germany, Austria, and Italy, I became exceedingly grateful for our differences and commonalities. Thousands of individuals worldwide liked visiting the same places we valued. Their expressions were priceless as they examined artworks at the Galleria dell'Accademia and Doges Palace in Venice, underscoring how art and music are stepping-stones for expressing diverse views peacefully. Leonard Cohen's "Anthem" is relevant here, especially the following lines:

Ring the bells that still can ring
Forget your perfect offering
There is a crack, a crack in everything
That's how the light gets in.

Treating others with kindness and compassion connected total strangers, even momentarily. Journaling enlightened me to think of those times I disparaged others. I didn't know the faults I perceived about others were my shortcomings. Unmistakably, I was looking at myself despite differences in skin color, ethnicity, gender, and other characteristics. My renewed mindset is superior to the "Energizer Bunny;" it's a gift that keeps giving!

The simplicity of smiling and saying hello to others didn't require much physical exertion, only admiration for each day and fellow human beings. As I reached out to hotel staff and others, they showed gratitude by smiling back. Asking them how their day was going added to cheerfulness. Interestingly, research shows kindness and compassion toward others aids in rewiring our brains and positively affects our bodies.

Much of my journaling reflected my dependence on others to meet my needs. From my first cup of coffee in Paris to the delicious salmon in Munich, I wrote about the laborious process and hardships workers face in both industries. Although I may never meet anyone in either occupation, there's an invisible bond uniting us. As I consumed the fruits of their labor, they addressed my needs and theirs.

We can be thankful for whatever is pleasing to our senses and emotional, mental, physical, and spiritual well-being. During our trip, I was incredibly grateful for meeting total strangers, eating delicious meals, seeing beautiful architecture, walking on narrow, winding streets, hearing birds chirping outside our Venetian hotel room, and experiencing a beautiful sunset in Austria. These daily experiences electrified and energized me and constituted a crucial part of our journey.

Gratitude doesn't always encompass happy, joyful experiences. Journaling allowed me to accentuate the travesty of homelessness and the sadness of seeing families sleeping on streets, in home-less shelters, tents, and cardboard houses in Paris and other cities. The refugee crisis throughout the world is heart-wrenching. For many years, I selfishly lamented my childhood. However, my Bronx experience doesn't even begin to parallel the lives of millions of impoverished people worldwide. I'm incredibly grateful for the food, shelter, heat, and other amenities my parents lovingly provided. Being thankful for what I have is a gift; it inspires humility and allows me to empathize with and assist those less fortunate. Exhibiting gratitude has the power to change lives despite life's challenges, including physical, emotional, and mental pain. Additionally, it encourages compassion, which aids in joining with those in need.

As in mindfulness practice, gratitude embraces a judgment-free attitude. For instance, a few days after returning home, I exercised an old habit by sitting in my living room, eating breakfast, and watch-ing the news. Unfortunately, I often became stressed or frustrated over what I heard and saw. One morning, however, the unexpected came: the cable provider was performing maintenance throughout our service area, resulting in not having access to cable television. I thought, OK, no sweat; I'll use the radio to access my favorite news station. Inadvertently turning to a different station, classical music lured me, and since then, I've listened to it as I enjoy eating breakfast. What a delightful experience! An unexpected gift resulted from not judging inaccessibility to cable news as good or bad. Unintentionally turning to classical music has led to peacefully starting my day. I simply listen to or read about news events later. Interestingly, classical music has supplied a splendid backdrop for writing *The Gift of Travel*!

During the trip, the practice of mindful gratitude empowered me to reflect on what each day offered. I better understood how many things I took for granted were gifts enriching each day. For example, feeling the breeze on my face when riding a water taxi in Venice, smelling the wonderful aroma of freshly baked bread in Salzburg, touching snow in Partnach Gorge, and relishing beautiful landscapes were terrific experiences. I also grasped the importance of expanding on these experiences after returning home. Living close to the Gulf of Mexico, Claudia, Lindsey, and I feel its gentle breeze in the early morning, walk on smooth, fine sand, and adore the sound and splendor of waves. Being surrounded by natural beauty, we hike beautiful nature trails, go boating, meet up with friends, and experience other outdoor activities. These pursuits and those we experienced in Europe, and other places we've visited, nourish our well-being and commitment to regard each day as a gift, even in the face of challenges.

Compassion

A simple smile is an act of kindness exuding compassion in any country; in my case, it complemented the show of gratitude in places visited. Smiling at others in an elevator and gladly complying with a family's request to photograph them added value to each day. Moreover, I often asked individuals what they thought of paintings and sculptures in museums. On one occasion, I smiled at an elderly gentleman at the Louvre in Paris. Although he seemed tearful and sad, he responded with a big grin. These small, yet kind actions, heightened my travel experience. Mother Teresa wrote, "We cannot do great things on this earth. We can only do small things with great love."

As I wrote about these small acts of kindness, I recalled the elderly gentleman spitting on me at the Nuremberg Christmas market. I'm sure seeds of compassion are inside us, but we often forget to nurture and bring them to increased fruition. In my journal entries, I wrote about the countless times I disrespected or disliked someone for what they said or some aspect of their behavior. I didn't consider they may have been having a difficult day or going through personal trauma. Ian Maclaren wrote, "Be kind. Everyone you meet is fighting a hard battle." These words are a rallying call encompassing attentive listening, empathy, and willingness to communicate with and comfort others in times of need. Our life stories, filled with joys and sorrow, invite us to join as one.

A person experiences life as something separated from
the rest - a kind of optical delusion of consciousness. Our
task is to free ourselves from this self-imposed prison,
and through compassion, find the reality of Oneness.

Albert Einstein

Communicating with the Filipino gentleman accentuated the significance of cultivating relationships through empathy and compassion.
Had I not intently listened to his experience in the Philippines during
the Second World War, I wouldn't have learned he faced some of
the same challenges as my father. Upon hearing his words, my eyes
teared and made for a memorable moment. His half-moon, darkened
eyes were like those of the housekeeper at our Venetian hotel. I
thought of how his and her wisdom was a compilation of seasons
associated with happiness, sadness, violence, and other life experiences. My understanding of and appreciation for the interrelatedness
of different generations continue to strengthen by the day!

The camaraderie I shared with the couple from Spain, the mother
and daughter at the Ratskeller in Munich, the couple from Italy, and
the young man from England showed how sharing common interests
and avoiding stereotyping fosters a caring attitude for ourselves and
others. Our thoughtful conversations revealed being grateful for
traveling, enjoying different foods, appreciating famous artworks,

and liking diverse types of music. Yet, at times, I could tell we felt sadness over some of the travesties occurring throughout the world. I'm sure we would have developed lasting relationships with more time to interact.

Labeling individuals and groups of people because of their ethnicity, race, and other traits separate us from them and often results in unnecessary hatred, racism, sexism, bigotry, and other negativities leading to emotional, verbal, and physical violence. People commemorating Christmas in the cities we visited did so in a season of peace; tourists and non-tourists enjoyed a borderless season of giving and sharing, primary ingredients of mindful gratitude and compassion. There were no walls, fences, or guards separating individuals according to specific characteristics. Thinking back, I'm grateful for the baby's crying on our flight to Paris. Perhaps his crying was a call to experience the present moment and value others, especially during the Holiday Season. Maybe we could build monuments commemorating the loving-kindness individuals have internalized and practice daily.

Interestingly, before the trip, I labeled certain sounds of large cities as loud and obnoxious. But, unbeknownst to me, I thwarted exhibiting compassion. In Florence, I became increasingly aware of ambulance sirens and emergency medical personnel compassionately treating those needing medical assistance. Beforehand, I often thought of sirens as another source of noise pollution; now, I'm grateful for their sounds because they express a desire to relate with those in need.

It's up to us to stress the long-term significance of non-violently relating to others and its positive, lasting effect on future generations. Even on a small scale, a renewed mindset paves the way for mindful, grateful, and compassionate communities synergistically influencing others worldwide through face-to-face interactions and other kinds of peaceful human endeavors. We can incorporate these transformative efforts in all areas of our lives.

As with mindfulness and gratitude, research shows exhibiting kindness and compassion toward others rewires our brains, resulting in deeper empathy skills. As members of humanity, we're connected to others, even total strangers. A simple handshake, or embrace, can unite generations, and signify living as one despite differences. Witnessing the diverse multitudes of people in places we visited opened my heart, eyes, and mind. I realized the "time to love," "time to embrace," and "time for peace" can embellish all seasons of our lives.

So, the answer to *What Now?* includes a lifelong commitment to personal renewal and inner transformation. We simply need to have faith and trust in our efforts as we leave footprints of mindfulness, gratitude, and compassion to present and future generations. Indeed, we all live in the same universe, making us members of a universal family!

Resources

The following authors are deeply committed to the application of mindfulness, gratitude, and compassion in our everyday lives. Some of their writings are spiritually guided, while others emphasize a secular approach. In some instances, there's overlap between both. I urge you to check them out, in addition to others!

Bourgeault, Cynthia. *Eye of the Heart: A Spiritual Journey into the Imaginal Realm.* 2020.

Hanh, Thich Nhat. *Peace is Every Step: The Path of Mindfulness in Everyday Life.* 1991.

---. *You are Here: Discovering the Magic of the Present Moment.* 2010.

Germer, Christopher K. *The Mindful Path to Self-Compassion: Freeing Yourself from Destructive Thoughts and Emotions.* 2009.

Keating, Thomas. *Open Mind, Open Heart.* 20th Anniversary Edition. 2006.

Kralik, John. *A Simple Act of Gratitude: How Learning to Say Thank you Changed My Life.* 2011.

Lama, Dalai. *How to See Yourself as You Really Are.* 2007.

Langer, Ellen J. *Counterclockwise: Mindful Health and the Power of Possibility.* 2009.

---. *Mindfulness*: 25th Anniversary Edition. 2014.

Neff, Kristin. Self-Compassion. *The Proven Power of Being Kind to Yourself.* 2015.

Nelson, Kristi. *Wake Up Grateful: The Transformative Practice of Taking Nothing for Granted.* 2020.

Rohr, Richard. *Simplicity: The Freedom of Letting Go.* 2004.

Thoreau, Henry David. *Walden and Civil Disobedience.* 2005.

Tolle, Eckhart. *The Power of Now: A Guide to Spiritual Enlightenment.* 1999.

Zinn, John Kabat. *Wherever You Go, There You Are: Mindfulness Meditation in Everyday Life.* 1994.

Made in United States
Orlando, FL
11 August 2022

20894027R00146